Copyright © 2008 Kris Tabetando
All rights reserved.

ISBN: 0-9809111-0-9
ISBN-13: 9780980911107

Visit www.booksurge.com to order additional copies.

Visit www.WiseSuit.com to share your favorite business and inspirational books with us.

WiseSuit Wealth Series™

THE WEALTH IN QUESTIONS
Audacious Insights in Success and Wealth

By Kris Tabetando

Copyright © 2008 Kris Tabetando All Rights Reserved.

To
my Mother and Father
who continue to nurture my brothers, sisters and I
with unconditional love.

CONTENTS

1. THE WEALTH IN OUR QUESTIONS 1
2. WHAT IS WEALTH? 5
3. WHY ISN'T LOVE OF DOING ENOUGH? 11
4. IS OUR SPIRIT IN OUR WORK? 19
5. IS OUR WORK OUR BABY? 27
6. DOES GOAL SETTING REALLY WORK? 35
7. WHY DO WE FIND IT SO HARD TO DO NOTHING? 43
8. WHY DO WE PURSUE SIGNIFICANCE? 53
9. IS MY TRUTH YOUR TRUTH? 61
10. WHY DO WE FEAR UNCERTAINTY? 69
11. WHAT DO WE REALLY HAVE TO LOSE? 77
12. WHAT IS OUR PURPOSE IN LIFE? 85
13. OUR MIND, OUR QUESTIONS—OUR LIFE 97

ACKNOWLEDGMENTS

A labor of love like this book is never created alone. I am eternally grateful to a number of people who have contributed immeasurably to creating the book you now hold in your hands.

I extend my deep gratitude to the incredible team at BookSurge for their priceless help: Roy Francia for overseeing the project; Lindsay Parker for coordinating the editorial team; Laura Matthews, my editor; Lauren Woolley and Helen Smith for overseeing the design team; and Erin O'Leary for getting things started.

I have been inspired by life and numerous teachers over the years whose lessons are dripping from the words in this book. These teachers are too many to list here but I acknowledge them all respectfully.

Finally, I thank my personal support system, my family and friends, who continue to provide me with all the love I need and allow me to be myself and do what I do.

1. THE WEALTH IN OUR QUESTIONS

Why do we need praise or recognition from outside ourselves? Why do we need society to give us a pat on the back for our efforts? Why do we accept certain rules laid out by society and blindly follow them without question? Why don't we do something just because we love doing it? Why must there be some ulterior motive, some material or social reward, for what we do? Do we really need goals? What is wealth? What is success? What is failure? Do we truly have anything to lose in life? Why does uncertainty generate negative emotions instead of positive emotions most of the time? What is our purpose in life? What does it all mean?

Each of us receives illogical and unconventional thoughts and feelings from somewhere. Depending on our beliefs, we may each have a different name for this source of messages: Universe, God, Intuition, Infinite Wisdom, Infinite Intelligence, Universal Source, Universal Spirit, Spirit, or some other name. The specific name we use doesn't matter.

Often, because of the noise of society's alleged wisdom that has been drummed on the walls of our minds, some of us can't hear clear messages from the source anymore. Or we do hear the messages, but because they often go against conventional wisdom and logic, we choose to ignore them. I'm getting better at hearing my messages and acting on them. But I must admit, the noise of society that has accumulated in me over the decades sometimes gets the best of me. I often buckle under the pressure from society and do what is considered logical. In other words, I choose to go against my inner wisdom.

The sole purpose of this book is to arouse that dormant but eternally wise part of us using one of the most valuable gifts we all have—the ability to question. When we don't know, we ask, we seek, we explore our lack of knowledge. We go on a quest to search for the meaning behind our life experiences. And we always have the answers, the wisdom, within us. So we ultimately return to the wise one within.

I will call this wise one *Spirit*, but you can call it anything you choose to call it. It is that part of us that we run away from because it is considered crazy by society. It is the part of us that carries and will always carry our unique wisdom within it.

Note that I say "unique wisdom." We are each unique. Therefore, what is true for you may not necessarily be true for me. And as such, my Spirit holds the keys to my success. In the same way, your Spirit holds the keys to your success. The noise from society attempts to impose its rules upon us. But society's rules will never work for our individual situation. We must learn to listen to ourselves. We must learn to listen to our Spirit.

We must learn to ask questions and listen for the messages that rise from within us.

Our Spirit carries our answers—our unique wisdom.

The primary method of conversation of the Spirit is through our emotions. We either feel negative or we feel positive about something that occupies our minds. Whether negative or positive, we must look into that feeling to harvest the lesson that we are meant to learn.

For instance, numerous studies have shown that over seventy percent of people hate their jobs. When we dislike our work, we feel unmotivated and burned out, and we even attract a kind of depression. Something within is telling us that our lives are meant to be a vehicle to do much more than we are currently doing. The Spirit within wants more out of life than rushing to get to work before 9:00 a.m., going through the motions at our jobs, and heading home at 5:00 p.m., in exchange for a paycheck. Our Spirit is telling us that we can and want to do more. It is our responsibility to explore the emotions generated by our situation and dig deep to extract the wisdom in our feelings.

It takes a courageous individual to listen to messages from the Spirit and act on them. It takes a brave soul to go against centuries of accepted social wisdom that has taught us the merits of a stable career, secure shelter and peer acceptance. The rationale is that if we do something abnormal, we may become the butt of jokes from our peers. Fear of criticism from peers is such a powerful force that it causes gifted people like us to stick with the status quo regardless of how miserable we feel. In other words, we believe that it is better to live with the misery that we know than venture into the potentially rewarding unknown.

The words in this book are meant to generate questions within us. The purpose is to question what we have accepted as fact. The method is to ask simple questions. If we can question some doctrines that we had accepted without prior examination, we instantly take a major step forward. The questions bring answers with them. Let's choose to question everything. We will always be surprised by what we uncover. We often discover that we hold beliefs that have been imposed upon us by family, friends, or the media. But remember, in situations where our family members or peers may have fed us negative beliefs, they were not intentionally trying to sabotage our success. They can only share what they have been taught by others. They share what they know, right or wrong. It is not their fault. We always have the power to look closely at a message that we receive from anyone and decide for ourselves if it is right for us.

It takes a high level of self-awareness to be able to stand back and observe beliefs that we have accepted. We sometimes think the beliefs are who we are. This often causes us to defend beliefs that may not even be beneficial to us. We consider an attack on our belief system to be an attack on ourselves. But we are not our beliefs. Our beliefs are separate from our true Spirit. We adopted the beliefs along the way, and we now live them without ever questioning their truth. Wouldn't you want to succeed—or even fail—based on beliefs that you chose rather than beliefs imposed on you by others? Let's start to question those beliefs today.

The words in this book are meant to generate questions within us.

We are each born with specific unique gifts for us to share with the world in order to reach our maximum potential naturally and easily. This is what we often call *success*. But society jumps in to convince us that we must act in a specific way and be somebody else in order to succeed in life. Obviously, this road to success is much more treacherous and brings heartache, since it takes more energy not to be ourselves. We constantly practice and attempt to learn how to become and act like this successful other person. Our natural self, our Spirit, is deemed not good enough by society. Ironically, we are sold incorrect information on how to become successful when we were born with the correct success formula within us. This is the irony of our relationship to success. We chase it when we have it right now. We always had it.

So all we need to do is question our truths. In this way, we can uncover and embrace our unique spiritual truth, and walk away from the adopted truth that we have accepted but is wrong for us. Our Spirit will tell us if some thought is really our truth or somebody else's truth that we have adopted.

The interesting fact about an adopted truth is that it loses its power once we examine it. It will inevitably crumble under investigation. We do not need to use tremendous effort to get rid of it. We do not need to fight with it. It will fade away on its own. When we examine an adopted truth, the questions that arise in us act like a torch shining light into darkness. Darkness gives way immediately to light. The adopted truth is the darkness. The questions are the light. The adopted truth only has power because it has not been examined. Our questions shine a light on it, and it begins to lose its power over us. This is the power in questions.

> **Adopted truth loses its power once we examine it. The questions that arise in us act like a torch, shining light into darkness.**

On the other hand, our unique spiritual truth or wisdom never fades. It is eternal. It becomes clearer under examination. Over the years, because of society's conditioning, layers of dust accumulate on the window of our Spirit. The questions that arise in us simply wipe the dust off the window so that we can see our innate wisdom clearly. The noise from society causes us to lose our connection to this wisdom. The questions that we ask ourselves re-establish this connection. This is the wealth in questions.

Our unique wisdom is always here with us. We just have to reconnect with it. It's like being born with a unique talent that we carry with us throughout our life. Whether we use and share that special gift is up to us, but the talent is always within us. It is our responsibility to explore it and connect with it.

> **Spiritual truth becomes clearer under examination. The questions wipe the dust off of the window so that we can see our inner wisdom clearly.**

As we embark on this journey, I'd like to state here that I'm not your motivational coach. I'm not standing on the sidelines cheering you on. I'm on this journey of self-exploration with you. I have questions myself, and I seek answers. My questions may mirror your questions. So I present them here for each of us to study.

On my own quest, I've discovered some timeless wisdom, which I share with you unconditionally throughout the book that you now hold in your hands. As we each absorb the words on this journey and questions arise in us, we simply have to explore the thoughts and emotions that they generate. These thoughts and emotions come from our Spirit, which holds our unique wisdom and our wealth. That is the wealth found in our simple questions.

2. WHAT IS WEALTH?

One of the most misunderstood concepts for a lot of us is the definition of wealth. That simple word *wealth* generates such intense emotions, positive and negative, within us. When we hear the word, images of large bank accounts, luxury cars, expensive clothes and huge estates come to mind. It's understandable since our dictionaries define wealth in terms of strictly material possessions. I have always found it fascinating that one simple word, which we as human beings invented, can bring out tremendously intense reactions in different people.

What are some of the beliefs we attach to this word *wealth*?

To some of us, the love of money (wealth) is the root of all evil. Wealth to many is a bad word. The pursuit of wealth is undoubtedly the ultimate sin. Sometimes, wealth brings images of scarcity: we don't have wealth, and we may never have it. Wealth is reserved for some other person who probably acquired that wealth unscrupulously. Because of that belief, we do not want to be like the wealthy real estate developer who tore down the local community center to construct a multi-story condominium building. We refuse to be unscrupulous, so we choose not to have a relationship with wealth or engage in any conversation about wealth. As we all know, it is taboo to discuss wealth in our society. It makes us all feel uncomfortable. Yes, the rectangular pieces of paper that we call dollar bills do have that kind of power over people. Basically, the word *wealth* is not welcome in our daily lives.

To another group of us, wealth is the obvious solution to all of our problems. With a big enough bank account, we can buy whatever our heart desires and forever be drunk with joy. We never need to work another day in our lives. We can just lie on a beach somewhere, sip a fruity drink adorned with a small umbrella, and watch life go by. With wealth, we can buy instant respect from other people. They would never dare question our opinions and decisions. After all, with wealth, we no longer need to prove that we are intelligent. We believe, in fact we know, that to amass tremendous wealth, we must have an incredibly high IQ, and other people will immediately recognize that. With wealth, we expect people to wait on us. Since we make more money per hour than they do, our time is obviously more important than their time. That's right, we know wealth can do all this for us. In a nutshell, wealth is the ultimate destination.

Then there are those of us who see wealth as basically good. Wealth or money is a vehicle to contribute to the betterment of the world. Wealth creates jobs for other people. In turn, the employed provide food and shelter for their families and support local business through their spending as consumers. Wealth creates new products and services that we can all enjoy. More importantly, wealth enables us to make significant contributions to help those less fortunate than we are. Wealth brings with it the potential to attack social problems such as disease and lack of food or education. For us, wealth is a means to nourish the world. It is not an end in itself. It is a means to many positive ends.

These are the most prevalent thoughts generated by the word *wealth* in our society today. Of course, we don't each necessarily fall neatly into one of the categories. We may have different reactions to wealth at different times in our lives. An unpleasant interaction with a wealthy individual may cause us to resent all wealthy individuals. But in the same vein, we seek and chase down opportunities to strike it rich ourselves. Another scenario is one in which we may believe that wealth can be used to better the world, but at the same time, we believe that we are superior to others who are not as wealthy as we are.

Suffice it to say, we may hold beliefs that place us in multiple categories at the same time. And these beliefs may change throughout the course of our lives. So let's please not judge any of these categories as good or bad. They simply are a convenient starting point for our self-examination.

I will use the word *wealth* on many occasions throughout this book, so let me give you my working definition. To me, wealth has many forms. The type of wealth that we have described so far is Financial Wealth. Financial Wealth enables us to acquire the material things that we enjoy. However, in addition to Financial Wealth, I will focus on the Spiritual Wealth, Mental Wealth and Physical Wealth that we have as human beings.

Wealth exists in many forms: Spiritual Wealth, Mental Wealth, Physical Wealth and Financial Wealth.

If we give love to someone, even if that someone is ourselves, we are sharing our Spiritual Wealth with this person. If we learn something from somewhere or someone, we acquire Mental Wealth. If we are physically healthy, we are blessed with Physical Wealth. We are each born with some form of wealth. But more importantly, this means that we are wealthy right now.

The Laws of Wealth work in the exact same way as the Laws of Nature. They must work in the same way because, after all, we do live in nature. That's why we call our human emotions and actions human nature. In nature, everything must flow freely in order for it to thrive. Everything in nature, whether living or dead, contributes to the environment to which it belongs. No participant in nature is an island. We all share the wealth we have, consciously or unconsciously.

For example, plants receive sunlight from the sun and water from rain in order to grow. These plants give us crops that we use as food. We purchase the food with money received from our income source, a job, where we perform some activity for our employers or customers. Farmers then use the money we give to feed their families and reinvest in their farmland to grow even more crops for us. Wealth, in all its forms, flows freely.

To put it simply, we give wealth to receive wealth. In order to love, we must be able to give love first. And we don't have to give love solely to a family member or friend. A genuine smile to the cashier at the grocery store is the act of giving our Spiritual Wealth, our love, to that person. That smile may brighten the cashier's day, and she goes on to provide exceptional service to customers all through her work shift. These delighted customers then keep coming back to purchase more groceries from her store. In this way, the store attracts repeat sales, and the cashier enjoys income from the store.

All this new wealth was created from the wealth found in a simple smile. Of course, there are a million other ways that giving this Spiritual Wealth, a smile, may benefit people who interact with the store. The basic message is that we have wealth to give right now. We don't need a large bank account to be able to perform that simple gesture. Wealth is in us to give right away.

Similarly, to receive knowledge, one must give knowledge. A teacher gives knowledge to a student. However, by teaching, the teacher usually gets clearer insights and learns even more than the student does. So the teacher gives and receives Mental Wealth.

In addition to our minds, we have been blessed with physical bodies that need us to care for them. Proper nourishment and exercise are vital ingredients for a healthy body. We must give these ingredients to our bodies. We can then use our bodies to perform the physical activities necessary to share our Mental, Spiritual and Financial Wealth with the world. And we can help others nurture their Physical Wealth by sharing proper nutrition and exercise information with them. Physical Wealth is just as important as any other form of wealth. Our physical bodies are gifts to us. We must cherish our bodies. We must feed our bodies with good food.

Financial Wealth is the form of wealth that stirs up the strongest emotions in most people. But Financial Wealth holds no special position above any of the other forms of wealth. It must be allowed to flow freely as well. It is created by giving some form of wealth, in something of value, to others, and accepting the financial gifts it brings.

Warren Buffett provides his investors with uniquely great investments for their money. Donald Trump offers luxury accommodations to his tenants. Oprah Winfrey shares inspirational messages with her viewers primarily through the medium of television. Bill Gates provides the software that enables me to type these words on my personal computer. Steve Jobs creates innovative devices, like the Mac and iPod, which bring excitement to millions of people around the world.

The list of successful people who have shared their unique talents with the world is endless. They give their Physical, Mental and Spiritual Wealth, and freely accept the Financial Wealth it brings. Financial Wealth is created by giving our unique wealth to others, in the form of a product or service, and freely accepting the monetary value that is given to us in exchange for it. As we noted in nature, this new Financial Wealth must, in turn, flow again freely.

During different monetary transactions, we play different roles. At the grocery store, we give the money we earned at our job in return for the wealth (food products) we receive. Or, if we work at the grocery store, we receive the money and give food to the customer for her nourishment. The Financial Wealth flows as freely as it should.

All wealth—Physical, Mental, Spiritual and Financial Wealth—must flow freely to grow.

We face problems and cause ourselves distress when we try to impede the flow of wealth. In nature, when air is not allowed to flow freely through a room, the room grows stuffy and may start to smell. In the human body, when blood is not allowed to flow freely and carry food and oxygen to different internal body organs, we become ill. In a marital relationship, if information does not flow freely between spouses, the divorce attorney's office may be the next stop. Similarly, a lack of information flow in a business relationship between business partners will inevitably cause problems. In our professional lives, if we do not share our innate gifts or talents, our Spiritual Wealth, with the world, we feel unfulfilled. Basically, wealth, in all its forms, must be allowed to flow. This is as true in nature as it is in our lives.

Impeding the flow of wealth happens most often in the area of finances. When we begin to believe that there's not enough money for us all tomorrow, most of us feel anxious and fearful. So we attempt to hoard what we have today. Big mistake. This is the mindset that creates poverty in our lives. We must give Financial Wealth freely and gladly receive it from others. It is abundant. The well will never run dry.

In the same light, we should never hoard any other form of wealth that we have. There will always be more knowledge to acquire and share. There will always be more love to give and receive. Our innate talents are eternal, and will never be exhausted. Once again, there will always be more money created from new ideas. Wealth is limitless.

I should emphasize here that I'm not implying that we need not manage our finances properly. Sharing our Financial Wealth does not mean that we need to go out and empty our savings accounts to give away money. Financial planning is obviously very important.

What the flow of wealth means is that we need to question our beliefs about wealth, especially the common misconception about the scarcity of wealth. If we unconsciously apply this scarcity mentality to our finances, it usually rears its ugly head in our approach to life as a whole. After all, we are the same human beings in all the different areas of our life. Maybe we hold back on sharing our love, our talents, or our knowledge with others in the same way that we hold back on sharing our money.

This mindset of scarcity may have been imprinted on our minds because we grew up in a financially challenged situation. As such, our thoughts always default to Financial Wealth being unavailable to us. Note that our thoughts inevitably become our reality. Therefore, these thoughts are most likely the cause of any financial challenges that we may face today.

Unless we question our beliefs, we will never overcome this limiting frame of mind. If we can just get past our narrow definition of wealth and any negative beliefs about wealth, we realize we have so much to give right now. We were born wealthy. We can give a smile, we can give a kind word, we can give knowledge, we can share our skills and talents.

Contrary to popular opinion, Financial Wealth is not created from Financial Wealth. We don't need money to make money. Financial Wealth is created from Mental, Physical and Spiritual Wealth. It is created from the flow of ideas, talent, passion and physical activity.

Once again, Financial Wealth is not created from Financial Wealth. We don't need money to make money. Financial Wealth is created from Mental, Physical and Spiritual Wealth. It is created from the flow of ideas, talent, passion, and physical activity.

All wealth must flow to grow. The other side of the equation is the ability to freely receive wealth. A lot of us find this challenging. We find it difficult, consciously or unconsciously, to accept wealth, primarily financial. We have images of greedy, rich people who just keep taking and accumulating money. This is another one of those beliefs that we need to question.

Why does money generate such emotion? Money is just a piece of paper or a coin. What did it do wrong? Of course, there are some unscrupulous rich people. But there are also just as many unscrupulous financially poor people. If we understand that all our wealth, including Financial Wealth, is meant to flow to and from us, we see money for what it is: a vehicle for creating more wealth for even more people. It's just one of many forms of wealth. Let's not feel guilty about accepting money in exchange for the value we offer the world. We can accept the money, and, in turn, serve more people.

In business, the rich businessman's wealth exists in the form of office space, computers, machinery, office supplies, and other tools that the employees use to serve customers in exchange for monetary wealth. The business provides jobs for employees who spend their money in the community, products for clients, and investment opportunities for investors.

Once again, we see how wealth flows to so many different people, as it naturally should. The flow of wealth in all its forms, Financial, Spiritual, Mental, and Physical Wealth, is not meant to be restricted. True wealth must flow. The truly wealthy person allows wealth to flow.

All wealth must flow to grow.

---

3. WHY ISN'T LOVE OF DOING ENOUGH?

Throughout life we are conditioned to believe that the ultimate reward is in the goal that we successfully achieve, and the journey toward that goal is a necessary evil. As children, we were trained to move quickly past the activity in order to get to its reward as soon as possible. Remember the lesson we learned at the dinner table: "If you don't eat your vegetables, then you don't get any chocolate treat for dessert."

This programming is no different in our adult lives. We all know and accept that we must "pay our dues" in order to enjoy some reward at some future point in time. Another popular mantra is, "No pain, no gain." We all believe that those who have achieved significant success must have suffered to get to where they are. So, if we want to achieve a similar level of success, we must persevere through a whole train of activities that we don't enjoy, because some day, when we're successful, we won't have to do them anymore. The underlying theme here is that this present moment in itself is not important. It is simply a means to get to a better future.

Why not enjoy the journey towards the dream as much as the dream itself?

I've always asked myself why most of us don't choose to enjoy the journey on our way to the goal that we cherish. Wouldn't that be a much better way of living? Living life today waiting for tomorrow is an arrogant way of living. How can we be so presumptuous to believe that we will be alive on that future date? What if we walk outside and get run over by a bus today? Doesn't it make more sense to enjoy the activity that we are performing while we are performing it? In this way, if we drop dead today, we would have enjoyed our final moments.

I apologize for being so blunt about our mortality, but it is an uncomfortable truth that we will all pass away. And none of us has any idea exactly when this will happen. So we should cherish every moment with which we are blessed. Every moment we have is a gift. However, most of us treat this present moment as if it were dispensable. Remember, today will never repeat itself. Never. It is forever crossed off of our calendar. No two days of our lives will ever be exactly the same. Each moment of each day is unique. Tomorrow doesn't really exist. Every moment in life is now. Tomorrow becomes now. We have been conditioned to run past the now as quickly as possible to that brighter tomorrow of our dreams.

Because we spend such a huge part of our daily lives at work, this phenomenon is most noticeable in our professional lives. Some people work today in order to get quickly to a blissful retirement tomorrow. The overwhelming majority of us are right now performing jobs from which we get little to no fulfillment. Why? We may be hoping that if we just keep plugging away, some influential higher-up will notice our efforts and give us the keys to the promised land of riches. That promised land could be a promotion up the corporate ladder, financial wealth, or just a pat on the back. Will it happen? It might. But the alleged promised land is usually no better than this present sad existence.

So why don't we choose to enjoy the process towards the goal? It seems to me that if we enjoy the process, we achieve levels of success that we can't even imagine in our wildest dreams. It is common to see people who have achieved huge personal success continue to work passionately every day simply because they enjoy the activity. They don't need to work another day of their lives. They want to work.

Examples such as Bill Gates and Warren Buffett, two of the richest men in the world, come to mind. They have each achieved what the outside world considers success, but they keep showing up to work. I guarantee that the primary reason for their huge success is their love for the activity that brought them that success. Their success is a by-product of this love.

Success is a by-product of love for the activity.

Experiences from my own life clarify this for me. When I choose to suffer through the present because I expect some reward at the end of the activity, the reward almost never shows up. If it does, it is never as fulfilling as I anticipated. The pot of gold at the end of the rainbow is a myth. The gold is in the activity, here and now. When I enjoy the activity, I am amazed by how many seemingly coincidental occurrences present themselves and lead me to incredible rewards.

Let's explore the widely accepted notion that successful people suffer to get to where they are. What we observe from the outside as struggle and perseverance is joyful activity for the successful individual involved. I don't mean to imply that the successful individual doesn't face challenges that she would rather not face. I mean that her passion for the activity makes it much easier for her to keep moving forward despite these obstacles. She enjoys the particular activity regardless of the monetary or social rewards that it may bring. As such, obstacle or no obstacle, she can't stop doing what she is doing.

If we attempt to copy her path, we will suffer because we may not receive the same personal fulfillment that she receives from the activities on the journey. As such, the obstacles that present themselves seem insurmountable to us, and more often than not, will crush us. We just don't possess the same power of passion to overcome these obstacles as she does.

The pot of gold at the end of the rainbow is a myth. The gold is in the activity, here and now.

I remember years ago when I first started working out at the gym. I knew it was going to be hard work, and that I would need to stay constantly motivated if I wanted to achieve the fitness goals that I had set for myself at the time. Does this sound familiar to many of us? Physical fitness New Year's resolutions that we somehow have to re-launch with every new year? Anyway, I had launched mine, and I decided I would do whatever it took to get to that beautiful tomorrow.

During the first few months, I worked hard and plugged away at the gym. I constantly tracked my goals to ensure that I was on target. Then, as happens with so many of us, my willpower gave out and I gradually showed up less at the gym. Then, I stopped showing up at all.

Don't despair; this story has a happy ending. For some reason I can't explain to you, I decided to toss out the fitness goals and head back to the gym. I decided to go in and simply enjoy a good workout that day. I did this again during my next visit. Well, it's been eight years and counting. I now can't *not* go to the gym. I love it. It's my physical and mental therapy. I enjoy the physical activity itself. I don't have any fitness goals or deadlines. I don't even remember what my initial fitness goals were. The physical transformation that has happened so far amazes me, so I'm happy to say that I don't care what those initial goals were.

Occasionally, someone would ask me what my workout routine is and how to do what I did. At the tip of my tongue are the words, "It takes years of hard work." But that would be a lie. I don't work hard at it because it's fun for me. I'm sure some people can stay motivated just using the power of their will, but I can't. Passion is my motivator.

Passion is a much more powerful motivational tool than willpower, drive or ambition. The simple lessons I learned here are the same ones we learn from success stories in any endeavor. Passion or love for the activity will attract success. Passion is so much more powerful than drive.

We may even ask successful individuals what the keys to their success are. They often say, "Hard work." They are being sincere. But it's not the same level of hard work that you and I would experience if we attempted to imitate that individual. We would work much harder—and be more miserable—if we didn't have the same passion as that successful individual.

Passion is a much more powerful motivator than willpower, drive or ambition.

The idea of doing something we don't love for some brighter tomorrow shows up in some widely accepted business practices as well. One major example is the concept of networking socially in business. We all know the scenario where we grab a cocktail at an event and attempt to generate conversations with people we would never speak to if it weren't required.

I know this sounds socially inappropriate, but it's the truth. Walking into a room and striking up conversations with strangers (or even business acquaintances) is hardly an exciting endeavor for most of us. We wouldn't do it if we didn't have to.

So why do we do it? That stranger could hold the keys to a big sale for our company or could provide a major boost to our career. In short, the conversation may be a means to an end. Because of this internal agenda, in some cases, we are not really talking or listening to each other. We are waiting for a break in the conversation, to move on, and speak to the next more important person, if we discover that this individual is not as influential as we initially thought. I know this may be uncomfortable to digest, but a lot of networking at conferences or seminars has this underlying tone to it. It is what it is.

I once attended a conference for the venture capital crowd. I was seated at a table chatting with three other attendees, when a well-dressed lady in a business suit came over, nodded "Good morning," and sat down in an empty seat at the table. After a quick round of handshakes and introductions, she proceeded to take out four business cards, and ceremoniously placed them in front of each of us.

I found it a little odd since we had met less than two minutes prior and, apart from exchanging names, we hadn't discussed anything at all. The other three attendees pulled out their cards and each gave one to her as well. Unfortunately, I had run out of business cards, otherwise I would have done the same. Once again, no real conversation had taken place.

To some of us, this interaction may be standard procedure. But let's step out of our conditioning for a few seconds. Why would strangers interact in this way? Each of the attendees was hoping that some opportunity, any opportunity, may arise from exchanging business cards. This lady, or someone she knows, might be of benefit to us. This absolutely makes logical sense. So everyone seemed interested in the title on her business card, but no one seemed particularly interested in the person behind the card.

This particular example is simply meant for us to question our conditioning. Isn't it a better idea to have a genuine connection with one person instead of covering all bases by placing our business cards in the hands of dozens of people to whom we only said "Hi"? What do we do with business cards that we receive from strangers at networking events? Let's be honest. If we didn't make a real connection with the person who gave us the card, we usually just throw it out. I know I occasionally don't even remember who gave me the card.

People connect with other people for various reasons such as sharing the same interests, beliefs or values. We can't force a connection with someone else no matter how hard we try. And we all know that, given a choice, people will always do business with people whom they genuinely like. No matter how much we try to fake a connection in a conversation with someone else, both parties know intuitively that there is no deep connection. We have all been part of conversations that we couldn't wait to end.

What does all this have to do with enjoying the activity? Well, we should enjoy the interaction with the other person for the sake of the interaction. Let's be there fully in that moment with the other person. Let's really listen. Not because we expect a reward but because we enjoy the conversation. If we don't enjoy it, let's move on rather than insult the other person by faking interest. Like in every other area of life, if we connect with someone fully in that moment, we get to enjoy a personal connection, and any social or monetary reward is a by-product.

So let's enjoy the activity just as much as, or even more than, the expected reward. Remember, we can't force enjoyment. We are either passionate about the activity, or we are not. If we are, time flies as we are immersed in what we're doing. We can't stop doing it. It is logical that if we are so engrossed in something that we can't help but do it, we will become good at it and generate amazing rewards. If we are not passionate about it, we keep looking up at the clock on the wall. We can't wait for it to be over. Needless to say, the work will bring little satisfaction and little reward of any kind.

But this is how most of us live every day. We take on activities because we believe that at some point in the future, we'll start to have fun. All we need to do is get through today. So we toil and keep looking up to see if we've made it to our destination yet. It's like putting a pot of water on the stove to boil. If we let it boil, it reaches the boiling point quickly. However, if we keep opening the lid of the pot to see if the water has boiled, it takes much longer to get there.

Note that I'm not saying that we shouldn't have a dream toward which we're heading. I believe that a desired goal is important. But let's choose to enjoy the journey as well as the goal itself. Let's not wait to have fun in the future. Let's have fun now.

A well-known fact is that our well-laid plans for getting to our dreams never pan out exactly the way we envision them. So let's not delude ourselves into believing that we can chart our course accurately. Instead, let's choose the course that will bring us enjoyment today. If we are having fun today, our Spirit will guide us, as life presents opportunities that we couldn't have predicted to get to our desired outcome. This is what every successful individual in any arena has experienced, consciously or unconsciously.

This is the magic that lies in loving the activity right now. The wisdom always lies in this moment. And no future goal will ever completely satisfy us even when we achieve it. We will have to set new goals. The journey is where the satisfaction lies. Let's choose to enjoy the journey above all else.

If we are having fun today, our Spirit will guide us, as life presents opportunities that we couldn't have predicted to get to our desired outcome.

A number of success coaches teach us that we must hold and feed the thought of our desired goal until it becomes reality and that we must always associate strong positive emotions to the goal in order for it to come to fruition. I agree that to bring any dream to reality we must think positively about it over an extended timeframe. However, if we love the journey to any goal, we will not need to expend any mental energy in applying positive emotion to that goal. The thought of the goal will come with its own built-in positive energy. And our love of the journey will feed this goal to its fruition. We don't have to force it. We are passionate—we just can't help it.

So if we ever find ourselves struggling to stay motivated in pursuit of a goal, we must question whether it's the right goal for us. Because if it is right, passion for the goal comes naturally. No effort is required.

For instance, I love writing. I often hear that to write a book, a writer must set personal goals and deadlines, and persevere to hit these targets.

I have never been able to do this. I write when I feel inspired to write. I enjoy the process. I'm always amazed at how much I write in one sitting when I'm truly inspired. Then before I know it, I have a whole book on my hands. Do I believe that it takes detailed planning, hard work and perseverance to write a book? Maybe that works for others. But it doesn't work for me. I simply enjoy writing. I write regardless of whether I'm sharing information with you or not.

I've cited a number of personal experiences in this chapter because I can only speak from what I live, and I would like to encourage you also to look at your life and examine your activities. Like you, I still have activities that I perform because I'm hoping that I can run through them to get to some other place. I'm slowly learning to question these activities and often get rid of them. However, decades of my conditioning are putting up a worthy fight as I attempt to do this. I hear phrases in my head like: *You've got to pay your dues; Hang in there; Plug away and it will all come to you someday; Don't burn your bridges;* and *No pain, no gain.*

It takes a tremendous amount of courage to break free from the wisdom of the crowd. But it is necessary if we want to live our own lives. We don't want to live the lives of our peers, family members, or even ancestors who learned and accepted this conventional wisdom.

A great quote from Benjamin Franklin puts the idea of living joyfully in this moment into perspective: "Do you love life? Then do not squander time, for that's the stuff life is made of."

Well, our time is *now*. How are we using our time? Are our activities dripping with love? If they are not, let's examine them. Let's choose to do things out of love. Let's do because we love doing. The future will take care of itself. It doesn't need our help. If we love doing, the rewards will be greater than our small minds can ever imagine. That's the power in loving the activity in this moment.

The question to ask is: Am I doing this because I love doing it?

---

4. IS OUR SPIRIT IN OUR WORK?

Every business or professional creation that stands the test of time has a spiritual mission attached to it. The mission brings out the human Spirit in an otherwise ordinary activity.

As humans and spiritual beings, we connect with this Spirit in the work. We respond to it. We feel the soul of the work. In any line of work, if the work has a spiritual core, we unconsciously react to the Spirit in the creation. We sense something unique and intriguing about it, something that we have not felt before. The creator expresses her Spiritual Wealth in her work. The work is an expression of her Spirit. Because we each have Spirit, we respond to another Spirit on a subconscious level.

For instance, we respond emotionally to a great acting performance in a movie we watch. The actress seems to talk to us beyond the words she speaks. We connect with the Spirit of the character she plays. We are human, and whether we believe it or not, we have a Spirit that can connect to other people beyond our five senses.

Movies are a good example because the rational brain is put to rest for about two hours. We simply respond emotionally or spiritually to a movie. We know that it's not real, but we laugh or cry as if it is. Once again, we connect with the Spirit of the work.

We sense something unique and intriguing about work that expresses the Spirit of its creator.

This is the reason why so many renowned artists in any art form (including business) speak about allowing their work to come together organically or naturally. For example, in basketball, Michael Jordan often spoke of letting the game come to him. In music, Quincy Jones speaks of leaving the door to the music studio cracked open to let God come in and walk through the room. These are different ways of saying that we must bring our untainted Spirit to our work. The Spirit must be allowed to come in and join the work in its own time. Then, magic happens.

This concept applies to every line of work. We are each meant to be artists in our chosen profession. Our work is our creative expression. This creativity exists whether we sell widgets or whether we sing for a living. The Spirit is about love. But we often leave love out of our work. We give the potential monetary reward or social recognition a higher priority than love. This makes our work cold, empty and unoriginal.

The reason why there's such intense competition in the marketplace today is that most of the work is almost identical. Few products or services are unique. Few products bring any unique Spirit with them. This happens when financial reward alone has been allowed to rule over the process of creating the product. We can tell instantly when a business has been set up by intelligent businesspeople, from some of the best business schools, with solid business fundamentals, and zero Spirit. Something seems stale about their product. The sales pitch sounds like every other pitch we've heard.

Conformity is the name of their game. We feel nothing special for their creation. It is just another one of many products in the marketplace. It is just another entry in the Yellow Pages. At this point, if we are potential clients, we shop around to find out which one of these identical products carries the lowest price tag. Price is our only logical reason for choosing one over the other.

This issue of conformity doesn't just rear its ugly head in the products and services in the marketplace. It is even more predominant in the people peddling these me-too products. The business executives all dress in the same fashion as every other executive in their industry. They drive the same cars. They speak in the same way. They engage in the same hobbies because everyone else they know is doing the same. We can easily replace one executive with another and there would be little to no behavioral difference. It is sad but true.

Conformity is often associated with the business world but it is alive and well in every arena, including the arts. The so-called "rebel artists" often dress and talk in the same way. They frequent the same trendy places. They jump on the bandwagon of the latest fads in their world. They work hard to be part of the rebel crowd. If all the rebels are doing the same thing, are they really rebels? I think not.

The need for human beings to follow the crowd is innate. Despite our human need for individual recognition, hence the obsession with celebrity in our culture, our need not to be seen as weird or eccentric is a much stronger force.

In our teenage years, if all our peers smoked cigarettes and drank alcohol, most of us picked up the habits, too. Our adult years bring a different kind of peer pressure. In a crowd, we don't want to stand out too much. If everyone in our world is dressed in navy blue pinstripe suits, we don't want to be caught in a white suit. If everyone in our world is dressed in faded jeans and vintage T-shirts, well, then, that's what we will wear, too. If everyone in our profession carries a BlackBerry, we need one, too. Conformity is a part of our lives.

A couple of years ago there was a reality television show on The Learning Channel called *Million Dollar Agents*. It profiled a number of salespeople from a real estate agency in Miami, which specialized in selling high-end real estate. The central character in the show was a renowned salesman and founder of the agency, Carlos Justo. For more than two decades, Carlos, originally a poor Cuban immigrant to the United States, has built his solid reputation and financial wealth as one of the leading agents in the Miami real estate market. He sells luxury properties to many of Miami's richest residents.

Carlos has a natural sales ability as do most successful real estate salespeople. And he loves his work. However, he has some unique traits: he wears brightly colored robes to work instead of the typical business suit; he meets clients over lunch at restaurants instead of behind a desk at the office; and he meditates with his staff every morning. His clients don't seem to mind his eccentricities since he is a genuine friend and consistently finds great homes and investments for them. The key to his success is he brings his Spirit to his work. He is not afraid to be himself.

This natural uniqueness, which we each have, brings with it one of the most overused words in business today: branding. A brand is supposed to have distinct characteristics that are difficult, and sometimes impossible, to duplicate. For example, Coca-Cola is a major brand. Even if we succeed in creating the same Coca-Cola drink mixture in a new soda drink, we can never compete with the power of the Coca-Cola brand. People will almost always choose Coca-Cola over our product. In a similar fashion, by being himself, by bringing his unique Spirit to his work, Carlos has branded himself and his business. No other real estate agency can re-create Carlos Justo.

The lesson here is we each have a unique Spirit that we should bring to our work. But the irony is that we choose to run away from it and become like everyone else. Then we have to compete with all the other players on that level playing field where we are judged based on the rules of conformity.

If we bring our Spirit to our work, we are the sole player on our playing field. We create the field. No one can compete with us on our terrain. No one can duplicate our uniqueness: our physical appearance, our speech pattern, our talents and our passions. This is the power of our Spirit. This is the power of our uniqueness. And the beautiful thing about it is, we are all naturally unique. We don't need to go out and acquire it from anywhere. It is within us right now.

If we conform, we compete with other players on a level playing field. If we bring our unique Spirit to our work, we are the sole player on our field. We create the field.

Other notable success stories bring the idea of the Spirit in work to life. Before Steve Wynn began developing casino resorts in Las Vegas, a casino resort was simply a big box with hotel rooms and a casino in it. Wynn loves art and architectural design. He teamed up with great architects to design his beautiful resorts and purchased invaluable works of art from masters such as Picasso to display for his patrons. Today, his most beautiful creations, such as The Bellagio and Wynn Las Vegas, stand proudly for all of us to admire and enjoy. Steve Wynn brought art, structural design and commerce together in a new and unique manner.

Similarly, before Steve Jobs arrived on the technology scene, computers were meant to be strictly functional machines. Jobs brought his passion for industrial design to computers. This led to the creation of the beautiful Macintosh computer, which Steve Jobs and Apple Computer gave to the world. One man's uniqueness forced the entire computer industry to rethink its stance on the importance of aesthetic design in personal computers.

Finally, Howard Schultz visited Italy in the 1970s and brought back a passion for the romance of the Italian gourmet coffee drinking experience to the United States. Today, as chairman of Starbucks, he is considered the spiritual leader of the company. He speaks of Starbucks's work as a mission to provide the best coffee experience to the world. The incredible growth of Starbucks around the world is a testament that millions of people all over the globe feel his passion—his Spirit.

These three examples depict individuals who have simply brought their unique Spirit to the office with them. We cannot duplicate what they have. And they cannot duplicate what we have within us right now.

No one can ever duplicate our Spirit.

The absence of Spirit in our work is a sad thing to witness. It happens when we look solely to the potential reward from our work. Please don't get me wrong: in business, proper market and financial analyses are absolutely essential to a successful business venture. But there must be something extra to raise the business above the sea of mediocre and disposable businesses that we often encounter. This only happens when we add our unique Spirit to our business.

Business plans are meant to incorporate mission statements. A mission statement goes beyond the financial rewards. It outlines how the business will contribute positively to the world in which it operates. But this aspect is usually ignored in most business plans, or the words on paper never truly make it into the daily actions of the business team members.

Unfortunately, most of us have not been blessed with the gift to paint like Monet or sing like Pavarotti. Most of us work in the corporate business environment, so this is where we must bring our Spirit. That's why I use examples from this common business arena.

Some of us have a hard time figuring out what even makes us unique. So many years of conditioning have made us believe that we don't really have anything special to contribute to the world. After all, hasn't everything already been done? No, it has not yet been done in that unique way that only we can do it.

Millions of books have been written, but a book that carries our unique words hasn't been written yet. It will never be written until we write it. Millions of businesses have been built, but none has been built that brings together our unique talents, energy and creativity. Only we can create that business. Millions of paintings have been painted, but none with the brush strokes that come out of our Spirit. Once again, only we can decide if we want to bring that painting into existence. It is our gift to give the world. But it is our decision whether to give it or not.

It is often difficult to determine our uniqueness, our Spirit, even though it is staring us in the face. We don't normally pay attention to the things that we do naturally and easily. For instance, if singing, public speaking, painting, or financial analysis comes easily to us, we assume everyone else can do it. It is not that difficult to us, so why would we expect the world to reward us for this simple task? We believe that no one in their right mind would exchange their hard-earned money for this thing that we created so effortlessly and with so much pleasure.

Our conditioning, illustrated in mantras such as, "No pain, no gain," has led us to the conclusion that we have to toil and sweat for any reward, financial or otherwise. In other words, if we don't work hard at something, we don't deserve the rewards for it. Another way of putting it is, if some creative activity brings us pleasure, then we can't possibly expect to be rewarded for it. That would be selfish on our part.

On the other hand, if we find something difficult or unpleasant to do, we give it our undivided attention since it causes us stress. Ironically, most of us give most of our energy to shoring up our weaknesses, and less energy to developing our unique strengths. We go through life trying to work on those areas that we deem are not as good as those of our peers. Or, we work on areas that we believe we should be proficient at because of our ambitions. If we hope to make the executive ranks at our company, and every top executive in the company plays golf, we go out to practice on the golf course, even if, deep down, we'd rather be somewhere else.

Here, we are once again playing on that level playing field against a whole bunch of competitors. We may do okay. We may even eventually become the top player on the field. But our Spirit is not present, and we become the top player among a bunch of Spirit-less mediocre players. Our prized position simply emphasizes that we did the best job in suppressing our unique Spirit. It means we have become exceptionally proficient at playing by the rules of the game. We never achieve our maximum potential this way.

We can only achieve our full potential on our own private field. On this private field, there is no competition. On this field, we have unique gifts that we are developing every day. On this field, we can't be mediocre. We are great. We shine bright. We can't help it. We love it. This is the field we want to play on—the field within us.

However, most of us believe that we should only be rewarded if we have put an inordinate amount of physical or mental effort into an activity. But, the true value is in the benefit that the world receives from our work. The amount of time or effort we put into the work is absolutely irrelevant.

Some of the most beautiful music in the world was created, naturally and effortlessly, in a few short minutes from inspiration that struck the artist. These musical notes have brought immeasurable pleasure to millions of people who listen to the music. The reward to the artist is in the value he provides to all these people. He would not expect to be rewarded for just the time or effort he put into his creation.

This is how we must value our unique gifts as well. If we can give a great speech effortlessly that inspires or educates people, it is valuable. Most of us place little to no value on our natural abilities. Well, these abilities are our gifts to share. They are worth a great deal to a lot of people. Let's share the gifts and gladly receive the rewards that come with them. If we find the activity easy and pleasant to perform, that's great because it brings us joy in doing it and also brings joy to the people who experience it. In this way, Spiritual Wealth flows freely to all of us.

If we find an activity easy and pleasant to perform, that's great because it brings us joy in doing it and also brings joy to the people who experience it. Spiritual Wealth flows freely to all of us.

So let's not be afraid to bring our uniqueness, our Spirit, to our work. Let's leave our unique fingerprints on our work. It is who we are. Let's express it in our gifts to the world. It is wrong not to share these gifts.

Too many people feel like empty shells and have lost their playful Spirit. They are like parrots regurgitating words that we've heard a million times before. They all look identical, wearing the same uniform of clothes that their peers wear. There is no intriguing element or surprise from them. We know what is coming, and we are bored. A part of our brain is turned off as we listen to them. Let's not be these empty shells.

When we meet someone unique, we pay attention. We listen to his every word. His Spirit excites our Spirit. All of a sudden, we wake up. We are in the midst of something different. The individuals that we admire in life are unique, hence our fascination with these people. They are not like everybody else we encounter. We would like to adopt their courage and be unique, too. Well, we can. Let's bring our Spirit to our work.

I recognize that disconnecting from the chains of the crowd is extremely difficult. An instant clean break from the norms of society that we presently live in may not be realistic. But the questions that we ask ourselves are a starting point on our journey away from the mediocrity of conformity. Just asking these questions is a step in the right direction. The questions will naturally guide us at the right pace as we make our leap forward.

Let's get off the level playing field with the rest of the competition. Let's get onto our own private field where there are no competitors. No one can duplicate our unique gifts. No one can duplicate our peculiar habits. In other words, no one can duplicate our Spirit. Let's find out what comes easily and effortlessly to us. Let's share these gifts with the world in a small way today. These small steps lead to giant steps.

One of the most beautiful things to experience is work that comes out of the expression of a human Spirit. A movie. A painting. A book. Any great product. Great service. We feel the Spirit of the creator deep in our souls. We experience the soul of the creator in the work. It is only fair that we also share our Spirit with those who experience our work.

One of the most beautiful things to experience is work that comes out of the expression of a human Spirit. We feel the Spirit of the creator deep in our souls.

---

5. IS OUR WORK OUR BABY?

This chapter is an extension of our previous conversation. I like the Hollywood concept of the movie sequel. So let's call this chapter the sequel to "Is Our Spirit in Our Work?" The word "sequel" sounds so much more exciting than "extension," don't you think? Anyway, let's talk a little more about creative expression through our work.

"What would I want to leave behind proudly, in the area of work, after I'm gone?"

This simple question above helps me eliminate instant gratification or get-rich-quick schemes that occasionally pop into my mind. It's a very powerful question for us to explore at any age. It brings the work that we would undertake, regardless of the immediate reward, to the forefront of our mind. If we are not passionate about our current work, we will not be proud of what we leave behind.

This simple question pushes us to re-examine our work life. If we are working at a passion, the question brings out the spiritual mission in the work. Our work then becomes a vehicle to truly serve other people. When we work on a spiritual mission, our decisions are not driven solely by our own short-term gain. We are forced to think of the broader benefits to present and future generations.

In this way of thinking, our work is our baby. When we have a baby, we nurture her. We wouldn't just sell her to the highest bidder who presents a check. Our baby is more important than money. This idea doesn't just apply to business owners who may find themselves in a position to sell their businesses. Nor does it only speak to professionals in the creative fields who produce works of art. Every one of us has a gift that we can and should bring to work. For a corporate employee, the baby is the service that the employee provides to the employer.

If our work is simply a cash machine that disburses dollars, our decisions are based on who would pay the most for our service or how quickly we can get paid. But when our work is our baby, we feed it with our Spirit every day in order for it to grow so we can proudly leave behind a piece of us. In this case, money is not at the top of our list of priorities.

In our work lives, it is often very easy for us to get seduced by short-term rewards. But if we are nurturing our baby, we see beyond the seduction of instant gratification. We envision the work that we want to leave behind after we're gone. Even if, before we pass away, we do hand our creation over to some other person, we still worry about how our baby is doing in the hands of its new parent.

Every piece of work that has stood the test of time, whether it is a business, a work of art, or a service, was built in this frame of mind. All the great businesses that have survived decades were built by sticking to the spiritual mission and ignoring the inevitable fads in popular culture. They were built by nurturing the baby—the business—over time.

When our work is our baby, we feed it our Spirit every day in order for it to grow so we can proudly leave behind a piece of us.

In the movie business, great actors often agonize over choosing movies with which to get involved. This is because the actor wants to leave behind a great résumé of movies of which he can be proud. His résumé is his baby. He wants future generations to enjoy the movies and cherish what he created. It is tough to make project choices when the work is forever on film for anyone to watch and criticize during and after the actor's lifetime.

Some other actors sign on to movie projects that can bring them that big payday while their star is hot. Ultimately, they lose their luster, and join the bevy of mediocre actors. History inevitably discards their work, and they make no meaningful contribution to the craft of acting.

Well, how do we feel about our work? Would our grandchildren be proud of our work? If our work provides an intangible service, would our grandchildren be impressed if they heard stories told about our work?

In the world of financial investing, many financial advisors tout the importance of stock ownership in order to build financial wealth, and they teach widely accepted concepts such as diversification. As such, many of us own different stocks.

Stock ownership and diversification are excellent financial wealth building tools, but we often forget what stock ownership is, at a basic level. Ownership in a stock represents ownership in the business that issued the stock. A stock certificate means that the holder is one of the owners of the business, which brings with it all the responsibilities and benefits of ownership. However, to many stockholders, their stock holdings are just pieces of paper that, due to advances in technology, can be quickly and easily bought and sold. Some stockholders have little to no knowledge of the underlying business. For many, there is a mental disconnect between the underlying business and its stock.

What does investing in stocks have to do with our work being our baby? Well, a business is not a piece of paper. A business is a living entity involving the people who work at the company, the products created, the customers it serves, and the communities in which the business operates. If we choose to invest in it, we acquire a stake in a living entity. If we feel nothing for the business, that is, if we feel nothing for this baby, why own the stock?

Warren Buffett is probably the world's most renowned stock picker. He has built his financial wealth by buying and holding great stocks primarily because he loves the underlying businesses. The stocks are his babies. Instant gratification is not his goal. It is easy for him not to get seduced by the lure of short-term profit because he understands and loves the businesses. To Buffett, the business is not just a piece of paper to be sold quickly to the highest bidder. It is a living, breathing organism with real people involved. He takes pride in helping to nurture this baby to its best self. Investing is his art form.

We build real financial wealth in stocks by holding them over the long term. We hold stocks over the long term if we can see past the daily fluctuations in stock prices. And we are more likely to do this if we view the business as a baby that will grow over time. If there aren't any businesses that we understand and feel this way about, we should not own any stocks. We do not need to own stocks. Let's not spend our money in the stock market in the name of wealth building just because a financial advisor tells us to do so. Let's invest our time, money, and Spirit only in our babies.

The best investment advice is investing in ourselves, in our education, in our minds, in our passions, in our babies. If our work is our baby, we bring our Spirit to it, and the work takes on a new heightened dimension. It is no longer just a job. It becomes our contribution to the world.

When we bring our Spiritual Wealth, along with our Mental, Physical or Financial Wealth, to our work, we give wealth to people who experience the work. Our wealth flows to them. In turn, we receive wealth, financial or otherwise, from them as well. And so wealth flows freely to all of us, as it naturally should.

When our work is our baby, we also begin to notice that life provides inspiration for our work. The experiences we have in life somehow find themselves in our work. We unconsciously weave our experiences into the fabric of our creations. Simple everyday interactions bring with them ideas that we incorporate into our work. A conversation, a scent, a news article, or a sight can trigger ideas that lead to a new or simply improved product or service that we can then bring to the world. So you can understand why we will never run short of inspiration as long as we are alive. Life keeps providing new ideas.

I experience this in my area of contribution. I only write about what I experience. The insights that I come across daily by living in our beautiful world are dripping from every single page of this book. My life inspires every word you read.

When our work is our baby, life provides inspiration for our work. We unconsciously weave our experiences into the fabric of our creations.

Because of the unique gifts with which we are born, we attract certain life experiences. Our particular gifts and skills enable us to extract particular lessons from these experiences. Someone with a different set of skills may have the exact same experiences that we have, but will not see what we see.

When our work is our baby, we work in Spirit and we add our unique observations to our work. When we work in Spirit, there is no separation between us and our work. We are one. So if our work is criticized, positively or negatively, we feel it deep within us. This is good because it shows that our soul or Spirit is in our work. Work is not just a paycheck for us. If we are just working at a job to pay the bills, criticism of the work doesn't affect us deeply or even at all. For as long as the cash machine dispenses the dollar bills, we don't care about anything else. But if our work is our baby, it holds our Spirit. We do care because our work is an expression of our Spirit.

Most of us often have two conflicting personalities at work and at play. Society even advises us to set this distinction. We separate ourselves at play from ourselves at work. We are trained to separate our work from our play. At play, we're supposed to be our true and relaxed selves. And, at work, we're supposed to be serious and professional.

The two main arguments for this are, firstly, that we need to have balance—otherwise, without clear boundaries, we might get overworked and burn out. And secondly, if we are the same self at work as at play, we might stand out as weird. These are very legitimate arguments.

We'll talk about the first argument regarding burnout later in this chapter. In relation to the second argument, I agree that we can't act around our co-workers in the same manner that we would act around friends in a social setting. It's probably a good idea to be slightly more serious around our co-workers. (Otherwise, don't be surprised if co-workers begin to recommend psychiatrists.)

However, what I refer to is not our physical activity; I'm talking about our spiritual activity. We don't need to leave our Spirit at home when we leave for the workplace. We don't need to turn it off at the office. If we are nurturing a baby, we can't turn off our Spirit consciously. Our Spirit is always on whether we are at work or at play. We are the same person at work and at play. In fact, the most successful people are the ones who never work. Work is play. There is no difference between the two.

This is why so many successful people keep working long after they have achieved what you and I consider ultimate success. The successful individual can't help it. She is just expressing herself through her work. It's like breathing. We can't possibly ask her to stop breathing and expect her to comply. She is simply having fun. Our society chooses to call it "work." The specific label means absolutely nothing to her. It may be work to others. To her, she's simply breathing. So she cannot, and should not, prevent her playful Spirit from infiltrating her work.

If we are nurturing a baby, we can't turn off our Spirit. Our Spirit is always on whether we are at work or at play. We are the same person at work and at play. Work is play.

A lot of ills are accepted in the modern workplace under the guise that people have separate identities at work and at play. We often hear the saying, "It's just business. It's not personal." This widely accepted doctrine implies that the individual who may have acted inappropriately is a somewhat different person in his personal life than in his business life.

In other words, under the same circumstances, in his personal life, he would have acted differently. This may indeed be true. Maybe he would have acted differently. But this also implies that when he walks into the office every morning, he must become a different person. He must move the switch to his Spirit into the off position. He can't possibly be himself completely at his place of business. He wouldn't survive in the corporate jungle. In order to survive, he must become somebody else. He must dress like that other person. He must talk like that other person. He must act like that other person. His true Spirit is not welcome at the office.

It's safe to say then that his true Spirit will not be a part of his work. We will never feel his soul if we interact with his work. His work will look and feel like something we've already seen. His work will be just another one of many in the crowd. Nothing special. Nothing unique. Nothing worth writing home about.

This scenario is all too common in our world today. This is how most of us operate in that part of life that we call "work." We believe that our work must be clearly distinct from our personal lives. We are each uniquely gifted people, with a unique Spirit that never makes its way into our work. It's unfortunate.

Proponents of work/personal life balance argue that we may get burned out if we are always working. Therefore, we must create clear boundaries between our work lives and our personal lives. Rather, I believe we don't get burned out from too much work. We get burned out from uninspiring work.

We get burned out when our work is just a cash machine. We get burned out when our work has no spiritual mission attached to it. We get burned out when we work to feed our ego.

We never get burned out when we are working in Spirit. We never get burned out when we are nurturing our baby. We cannot get burned out when we are simply being ourselves through our work. We cannot get burned out when we are simply breathing.

When we are working in Spirit, we are the same person in our work and personal lives. The switch to our Spirit is always turned on, whether we are at a family dinner or at a board meeting. We are one and the same person.

We don't get burned out from too much work. We get burned out from uninspiring work.

If our work is our baby, we work in Spirit. We obviously should be fully present, mentally and physically, when we are with family. But remember, when we're with family, we don't have to be consciously thinking about work for our personal lives to inspire our work. Simple interactions at home can trigger great ideas that we can incorporate into our work. A simple conversation with a child can start a chain of thoughts that leads to new ideas for work. This simple way of living will never create burnout.

There is no rule written anywhere stating that creativity turns itself off the moment we walk out the office door at 5:00 p.m. In fact, to be successful in our work, we must get rid of the notion of nine to five. If we want average results, we can work the average nine to five hours. Please note once again that I'm not just talking about physical activity. We don't have to be present physically at the office to nurture our work, our baby. Flashes of inspiration can present themselves to us at any hour of the day. These flashes are just as or even more important than the physical activity we perform at the office.

Our Spirit doesn't turn itself off. But if our work is just a cash machine, our Spirit can't contribute, so we invariably suppress it, and it stays dormant. In so doing, we welcome the mediocre into our work. If our work is our baby, we never settle for the mediocre. We bring in our Spirit to nurture our baby to its highest potential.

If we discover that our work is not our baby, then we must keep on searching to find work that we want to nurture, like a baby, to its greatest potential. If our work is our baby, reminding ourselves of this helps us to ignore the puppy called "instant gratification" that sits outside our door waiting to be let in.

For instance, we may make millions of dollars by selling our business today, but do we really want our baby in new hands? Would our baby be better off with those new parents than it is in our care today? These are the questions that pop into the mind of any businessman who has nurtured his business, his baby, over a long time, and is presented with the opportunity to sell.

To a businessman who views his business simply as a cash-generating asset, the answer is simple and straightforward: Sell to the highest bidder. The businessman who loves his baby, wavers and worries about the decision he has to make. This is more than just money to him. Parting ways with his baby is no simple feat.

We often hear that we need to remove emotion from our business decisions. But this emotional connection between the businessman and his business is the powerful engine that keeps businesses going through the tough times. Faced with obstacles, the businessman does whatever it takes to keep his baby alive. This is exactly how the businesses that we admire were built.

So let's not fault the businessman for the emotions fueling his indecision about whether or not to sell. Let's understand and learn from his predicament. His creation is his baby. This somewhat paternal connection enabled him to build a business that others see value in and for which they are willing to pay. He may make the right choice or he may make the wrong choice about selling. It is not our place to judge. It's our place to learn from the passion he has for his work, the passion he has for his baby. Do we feel the same way about our work?

We often hear that we need to remove emotion from our business decisions. But the emotional connection between the businessman and his business, his baby, is the powerful engine that keeps businesses going through the tough times.

At the beginning of this chapter, we explored the question, "What would I want to leave behind proudly, in the area of work, after I'm gone?" This question does eliminate get-rich-quick schemes. But we must be careful because sometimes the idea of leaving behind a legacy may bring out the ego in us. Sometimes we seek immortality through our legacy. Our legacy is our way of making sure that we are never forgotten. And because of this, we may make decisions today that are not beneficial to others. We may force our inheritors to handle our legacy in ways that are not necessarily in their best interests.

So we need to be honest and ask ourselves if we can live with the possibility that someone will come in and take our work in a different direction. Or even that someone will come in and destroy our life's work to make way for something new.

Because ultimately, our work must change with the times. Change is constant. What is relevant today may be irrelevant tomorrow. Breakthrough technology today is obsolete tomorrow. If we can live with change, we understand that we don't own anything. As creators, we are just custodians of our creations while we are alive. We must do our best to give our Spirit to our work while it's in our custody. What happens to our baby after we are gone is out of our hands. If our work is our baby, we will have no problem giving our entire Spirit to it, and we'll leave behind something about which we can be eternally proud.

Let's commit today, right now, only to do work that means something significant to us. Let's commit to invest ourselves only in our babies.

---

6. DOES GOAL SETTING REALLY WORK?

Thousands of books have been written on the subject of goal setting and its importance to success in any endeavor. Almost every success coach teaches the benefits of each of us setting specific goals toward which to work. These goals must be given a timeframe within which we intend to bring the goal to fruition in physical reality. As such, a specific goal and a specific deadline for its achievement are predominant instruments in the toolboxes of most of us who want to achieve anything in our lives.

There are many specific goal-setting techniques that have been developed and shared with the world. Some techniques involve writing the goal and deadline down, then looking at the written statement just before we go to sleep at night and immediately after we wake up in the morning. At night when we go to sleep, our rational or conscious mind goes to sleep and our subconscious mind goes to work to find the appropriate path for us to bring the goal to fruition in the stated timeframe.

Our subconscious mind is that part of our mind where we receive messages in the form of intuition. In order for the subconscious to function optimally, we need to quiet the chatter of our rational mind. The rational mind churns out thoughts all day long and quiets down when we go to sleep. This is when the subconscious can work its magic. In the morning, immediately after we wake up, our rational mind is still not fully awake, and we once again have the opportunity to re-supply the goal and deadline to the subconscious. In this way, it can attract opportunities throughout our day that lead us closer to manifesting the goal.

Another method used by some people is they carry the written statement or image of their goal around with them all day long. The idea is that the goal is kept at the forefront of the mind, not just in the morning and at night, but also throughout the day. In this way, once again, it feeds the mind, which in turn attracts opportunities to bring the goal to reality.

These are just two of many goal-setting techniques out there. Most of the other methods are variations of these two techniques. They are built around the same concept of feeding the goal to the subconscious mind regularly, and the subconscious will attract the circumstances necessary to bring the goal to physical reality.

Before I offer my opinions on the concept of goal setting, I should say here that I have never used any goal-setting technique successfully or unsuccessfully. My past experiences with goal setting followed one of the following three patterns. If I did set a goal, I had a tendency to end up in such an unexpected place that I didn't remember what my initial goal was. In some cases, I completely lost interest in the specific project and goals on which I was working. In other cases, my desires changed as I moved along towards an earlier stated goal, and I didn't explicitly set any new goals. Today, I work on my mindset and then follow the nudge of my intuition. So this is my experience with goal setting.

There are six billion people on the planet so I'm positive some people have had different experiences from mine. In this way, my opinions on the matter may not be in line with theirs. As with every other conversation we've had in this book, I share my insights with you in order that you examine your beliefs on goal setting, truly question them, and decide for yourself where you stand.

A common goal for many people is financial independence. So many of us dream of that blessed day when we have enough money in the bank that we can tell our employer that we will not be showing up to work tomorrow morning—that blessed day when we no longer need to work. We work only if we want to. We work only on projects that really fulfill us.

Financial independence is such a prevalent goal on many minds that it is an ideal example to explore. Each of us has a different dollar amount that represents financial independence to us.

Let's take the common notion of making one million dollars. To some people, this means making one million dollars in pre-tax income in a given year. To others, it is one million dollars sitting in our bank accounts waiting for us to decide where we want to spend it. Either way, one million dollars seems to generate highly emotional images in most of us. So let's explore the goal to make one million dollars within any timeframe of your choice. Different people have very different goals so, by all means, you can insert your specific goal in place of this one million dollar goal.

What are the possible future outcomes here? Well, the most desirable outcome is that we make our million dollars within the timeframe we set, and then we set a new, higher goal. The other side of the coin is that we don't make our million dollars at all. In fact, the time deadline we chose has passed us by; we are still living paycheck to paycheck and barely paying our bills on time.

These are the two potential extremes of success and failure. In success, most of us would ask ourselves questions such as, "How did I accomplish my goal, and how can I repeat the process to achieve even higher levels of success—say, two million?" In failure, we may ask ourselves, "How come, despite my hard work and all my efforts, I could not achieve my goal?" These are obvious questions. But I believe that we need to begin the examination before the goal is set in the first place.

Why did we set that specific goal?

Why one million dollars? Why do we have a fascination with that specific dollar amount of $1 million? Why not $1.3 million? Why not $10 million? Why not $100 million? Similarly, if your goal was different from $1 million, ask yourself why you chose that specific number or that specific goal.

The most reliable answer is that we have been conditioned to believe that one million dollars, or whatever our goal is, will bring with it that lifestyle of which we dream. The conditioning may have come from our peers, from our family, or from the constant barrage of information we receive through television, magazines, newspapers, or the Internet. The word "millionaire" is celebrated as a designation that we all need to strive to acquire. Remember, there's absolutely nothing wrong with achieving this millionaire status. Financial Wealth is just as important as Mental, Spiritual and Physical Wealth. But it is imperative that we understand where the meaning came from that we attach to "millionaire."

If we take a moment to think about it, the Universe that steps in to work with our subconscious mind to bring our goal to reality doesn't care whether the goal is $1 million or $100 million. So we could settle on either one as our goal, and, if the goal-setting technique truly works, we would achieve it. As such, if we analyze this logically, the goal-setting technique plays its role perfectly. Therefore, everything being equal, the only reason why one goal is achieved over the other is the person who set the goal—the *goal-setter*. By setting that specific goal, we limited our own achievements to what we deemed is a realistic goal.

Why would we choose one goal over another? The answer is because of the conditioning we have received throughout our lives. If, as the goal-setter, we choose $1 million over $100 million, it is because our mindset, developed through everything we have learned over the course of our life, tells us that, with hard work, we have a more reasonable chance of achieving $1 million than we have of achieving $100 million. $100 million is not reasonable to us.

Remember, I repeat, the Universe can't tell the difference between $1 million and $100 million. It works towards any number we set for it. By settling on the widely accepted benchmark of wealth, our reasonable goal of $1 million, we eliminate any other possible outcomes. The Universe begins to work to bring opportunities to us for us to achieve the goal of $1 million. All of a sudden, we have narrowed our otherwise unlimited potential down to a single number.

This implies that someone else with a different mindset, developed from different conditioning, would set and potentially achieve a different goal. If that other person sees $1 million as unrealistic, they may set their goal at $100,000. Or if that person views $1 million as too small, they may go for $10 million. However, the bottom line is that neither one of the two of us is superior to the other. We simply have different belief systems about what we can, and want to, achieve.

So it seems to me that even if we both achieve our respective goals, we may have each shortchanged ourselves unconsciously. The Universe is sitting around waiting for us to ask for more and, because of our belief systems, we settle for less. If the Universe doesn't spend any more energy bringing either $1 million or $100 million into our lives, why settle for either one of the two options?

The Universe is sitting around waiting for us to ask for more and, because of our belief systems, we settle for less.

I've used Financial Wealth in this example because it is such a common target for a lot of people. But this theory applies to any goal, financial or otherwise. If a young man comes from a family where no other family member ever went to university, graduating from university is a major accomplishment in his family, and rightly so. On the other hand, if there's a young lady who comes from a family where everyone received a university diploma, she is expected to do the same by her family. The family history in each case provides different mental conditioning to each of the two young people. There is no doubt that each of the two has the intellectual ability to acquire a diploma. The only limit is in the mind of the individual.

Each of the two young people has the seed of something much bigger than a diploma. The conditioning of the young lady enables her to automatically see beyond the diploma. The young man has to work harder on his mind to view his prospective diploma as a small step in his journey instead of as the zenith of his accomplishments. Once again, this all results from the conditioning they each received. The conditioning leads to different goals. But, again, the Universe brings whatever each requests. Will their conditioning limit the goals they set for themselves and, ultimately, limit their huge potential?

Many people who have achieved any notable success in anything remark repeatedly that their achievements surpass their wildest dreams. Our dreams result from our conditioning, so our dreams have the power to limit us. We break our dreams down into goals. Our goals are images of a brighter tomorrow. So unless we can see past our conditioning, we limit our full potential. The only way to see past our conditioning is to live in this moment today.

The wisdom we seek is available in each moment right now. Reaching our full potential is not some ambition or future goal. We have to attempt to reach our full potential every moment. We need to listen to the wisdom of the moment. Everything we experience emotionally or physically, positive or negative, is meant to teach us something in that moment. We have to examine it and pull out the lesson. It is hard to do this when we are living the experience. But just being aware that there is wisdom in the occurrence is enough. Eventually, living the wisdom in all these moments adds up to a future that we can't possibly imagine. This is our full potential. It is always here now.

The problem with having a specific goal is that it gives us the false impression that if we achieve it, we reach our full potential in that moment. Please don't get me wrong, having an image of what we would like to achieve tomorrow is a great idea. It provides the fuel that we need to get started on our journey today. But let's also entertain the possibility that the image we have may be too small and narrow. Let's contemplate the notion that if we leave the Universe alone, it would bring something much bigger into our life.

This is the problem with today's goal-setting strategies. They usually limit our potential when we set very rigid and specific goals and deadlines. Maybe the goals will manifest as planned. Maybe they will not. But the problem is that we begin to make decisions in each moment based on the schedule that we have set in place for the goal. As such, we no longer hear the wisdom in each moment. If we just enjoy this moment and extract the wisdom from it, our minds would eventually come to see that the goal that we set is puny next to what we can accomplish.

All wisdom lies in each moment. Our unique truth lies in each moment. If we just listen, each moment carries beautiful questions and answers. Goals often provide answers before we even have the chance to hear the question. We have already decided what the end looks like. We ignore any new information in the moment.

Each moment brings questions such as, "What do I do in this situation?" If we hear this question, and we already know where we want to end up, we often basically work backwards from the goal to the question. The answer we choose is the answer that provides a logical step towards the goal. On the other hand, if we eliminate the future and just focus on the present, we may find a completely different answer. This answer may not provide a logical step towards the goal. But the ultimate by-product of being aware of wisdom in each moment is a brighter future than our limited goals can provide.

> **If we just listen, each moment carries beautiful questions and answers. Goals often provide answers before we have even had a chance to hear the question.**

The ideas here don't cohere with the modern goal-setting theories that emphasize we should focus on a specific outcome until it is manifested in physical reality. So this may sound strange and even unacceptable to many of us.

In nature, plants and animals don't need goals to reach their full potential, so why do we? Plants and animals just grow naturally to their optimum potential. As children, we had no goals. We lived entirely for the moment. We always reached our full potential in that moment. As we grew into adulthood, we quickly dismissed this as naïveté instead of seeing the pure untarnished intelligence in it. The reason for this is, as adults, we have a choice. I ask that we use our choice and examine the possibility that we may not need specific goals.

This has applied to my life in small and large ways. I have achieved some things that my small mind could never have imagined. For instance, writing this book was never a goal of mine. Life provides these words to me, and I place them on these pages. I'll repeat again, the Universe doesn't care about the size of the undertaking. It will work with us whether we are looking to open a convenience store or build a multibillion dollar business. Once again, the only difference is in the mind of the individual. To one individual, a successful convenience store is a huge accomplishment. To another individual, one multibillion dollar business is just a small step.

When we let the Universe work with our full potential, we achieve something much bigger than we envisioned or we achieve something completely different from what we set out to accomplish. In business, so many ventures start out in one line of business and ultimately become huge successes in completely different areas that the managers never laid out in their business plans. We can't control the future. We can only live fully in this moment.

So am I saying that we definitely need not have any goals at all? Personally, I focus on building my mindset, which builds images of a desirable future in my mind, but I have no specific goals or deadlines. The goal-setting techniques taught today emphasize that we focus all our attention obsessively on a specific goal to be realized in a specific timeframe. This inflexibility severely limits our true potential. We could achieve so much more than fixed goals.

I must also add here that I don't believe any of us can, or should bother to, consciously eliminate images of a desired outcome when we take on a new challenge. We are human, and expectations or images of what we'd like to have happen in the future will inevitably pop into our minds. We can't, and shouldn't, resist these images. Let's enjoy our desired images—they fuel our lives—but let's redefine the concept of goal setting as we know it.

Instead of fighting against our goals, which are our own creations, let's understand their place in our lives. We always seem to need some future reward to peel us off of our couches in order for us to go out and start something. This reward may be financial, social, or personal.

Goals are useful tools because they provide the motivational energy we need to get started and keep us moving forward. But we must realize that our potential always lies in something bigger or completely different that may present itself as we make our way toward our goal. Let's not get obsessed with the notion that we must set and achieve our rigid goal within our rigid timeframe. A sudden new opportunity may lead us to greater heights and immeasurable fulfillment. Let's not let the noise of the goal prevent us from listening to our Spirit.

Let's explore the wisdom within an unforeseen opportunity. It may not lead us anywhere physically. We may examine it and choose to ignore it. But it always carries spiritual wisdom within it. It will always lead us somewhere spiritually. So, by all means, let's have images of what we'd like to have happen, but let's always remember that a better proposition may meet us along our journey. In fact, the Universe always presents a better path. It knows what we don't know. It sees what we can't see.

Let's not get obsessed with achieving that one rigid goal within the chosen timeframe. Let's not let the noise of the goal prevent us from listening to our Spirit.

We tend to plan in linear fashion. We plan to move from A to B to C. However, life doesn't follow a linear path. In life, we may move from A to E to Z and back to A. Our small minds can never predict this path because it's not logical. For instance, someone might take twenty years to achieve financial independence. Another person may achieve it in a year. Logic says that financial independence comes over the longer timeframe. But the Universe, in conjunction with the individual Spirit, works on its own time and in its own way. It doesn't care about our logic. Neither one of the two people is superior to the other. Each person is unique. Each has his own lessons along his unique path.

All we have to do today is study the mental conditioning that leads to our goals. And let's look at our goals, too. Let's listen to what our Spirit tells us about our goals. If we feel that a goal is not right for us, let's not be ashamed to rid ourselves of it. It doesn't make us a failure. It doesn't mean that we are no longer ambitious achievers. It simply means that we have listened to the wisdom in that moment and decided not to nurture that goal. We know that our Spirit will show us where we can put our huge innate potential to much better use. If we do decide to stick with some fixed goal, let's remember that it may be too small for all of our massive potential. Along our journey, we may get new instructions from our Spirit leading us down a better path. We must listen to our Spirit.

This conversation is meant to generate questions within us. If our questions lead to answers that bring us back to what we are already doing, then that is a good thing. This means that we have questioned our conditioning, our thoughts, and our actions, and decided that we were right after all. The questions have reinforced our beliefs. That, in itself, is rewarding.

Questions are important. The questions bring answers with them. But we must listen closely to make sure that the voice providing the answers is our voice and not the voice of someone else. Once and for all, let's identify the person behind the voice. Let's not blindly accept goal-setting techniques as they are widely practiced today just because some authority figure tells us to.

Let's see goal setting for what it is: a motivational tool that we use to get our engines started and to keep us moving along. It is a tool in our toolbox. We control the tool. We should never let the tool play the role of the master by allowing goals to take control of and become an obsessive fixation in our lives.

We have the power to override a goal if it no longer serves its purpose. We have the power to get rid of a goal entirely if some better opportunity presents itself, regardless of whether this leads us away from the initial goal or not. Our Spirit always knows best. Let it guide us in each precious moment.

We should never let the tool play the role of the master by allowing goals to take control of and become an obsessive fixation in our lives. Let our Spirit guide us in each precious moment.

---

7. WHY DO WE FIND IT SO HARD TO DO NOTHING?

We live in a society where we're always on the run, both mentally and physically. Each weekday morning, we rush to work. At work, we rush through our daily activities. At the end of the workday, we brave traffic as we make our way home. (It's called "rush hour" for a reason.) After work, we go out with family or friends, or stay home, have dinner, and watch television. Then, when fatigue sets in, we retire to bed. In the morning, we once again go through the whole process. On the weekends, many of us have a laundry list of things that we absolutely must get done before Monday comes around. And Monday is very reliable. It never shows up late, and once it presents itself, our original cycle continues.

In this cycle, most of us never take the time to be still and do nothing. At home, I often feel like I should be doing something, anything, right now. I sometimes find it difficult to sit and do nothing.

When we are extremely busy, we pray for a few moments of silence alone with ourselves. But when we do get this quiet time, and we all do get it despite our arguments to the contrary, we find something, anything, to do other than sit quietly with ourselves. The ability to be silent is a rare quality. Most of us can't do it. Or rather, most of us won't do it.

By silence, I mean mental as well as physical silence. Sitting on a couch and watching moving images on a television screen is not silence. Reading a tabloid magazine is not silence. Mental silence is being totally present here and now with no internal distractions. This means neither thinking about what we're going to do tomorrow nor going over an earlier occurrence in our mind. Silence means thinking neither about the past nor the future.

A lot of the time, most of us are physically here but mentally someplace else. It's almost comical. At work, we think of what we need to get done at home. At home, we think of what we need to get done at work. Then, we rush through our busy lives at work and at home, and regularly wish for a quiet moment to ourselves. And what happens when we do get that moment? We immerse ourselves in the book we just purchased, we watch TV, we pop a movie into the DVD player, or we grab a magazine to see what our favorite celebrities are up to today. The underlying pattern here is that we seek any kind of mental stimulation that would erase boredom.

True silence means, all of a sudden, we have to spend time with ourselves. We have to look within ourselves for entertainment. We have to look within for mental stimulation. We have to take a hard look at ourselves. Most of us find this incredibly uncomfortable. We need to be doing something. Therefore, we do absolutely anything not to have to endure the pain brought on by silence. We look outside for entertainment.

> **We seek any kind of mental stimulation that would erase boredom. True silence means, all of a sudden, we have to spend time with ourselves. Most of us find this incredibly uncomfortable.**

This basic human fear of silence is the driving force behind the entertainment industry. It is a big reason for the obsession with celebrity in our world. It is the reason for the growth of the phenomenon of reality television, where we watch ordinary people live their lives. This fear is just as intense today as it has ever been. We would rather immerse ourselves in the life of that other person, that celebrity, than live our own present reality. What the other person is living seems to be much more fun than our boring existence.

This is also the reason why there will always be the so-called "cool kids" in every school. For some reason, we need people to watch. We need people to make us dream. We believe their lives are exciting. We'd like to have the great lives that they have. There will always be cool kids in schools, and in the same vein, there will always be celebrities in the world. After all, in the same way that kids create the image of the cool kid at their school, we create the celebrity. The celebrity is a celebrity basically because we are fascinated by him or her. We will always be fascinated by certain people for any number of reasons. We create the celebrity in our minds.

I present these facts here so that we don't bother to fight against this human trait. Let's simply explore it and see what insights arise from it. When we face prolonged silence in our daily lives, most of us instinctively attempt to step into the life of some other person. The remote control, magazine, computer, book, or movie theater make this so easy.

Some people keep themselves busy with physical activity in order to run away from silence. We chat with friends over the phone, over the Internet, or over drinks. We build things around the house or busily clean our homes. The physical activity takes the mind off of the silence. In a nutshell, people would do anything not to have to be silent with themselves.

The question "What are you doing?" is very common. And a common answer given by most people is "Nothing." But nothing doesn't really mean nothing. Nothing may mean "I'm watching TV," but since it's a passive activity, I believe I am actually doing nothing. Nothing may mean, "I'm flipping through a magazine."

Throughout this chapter, when I speak of doing nothing, I mean sitting still and enjoying the silence of this present moment. Despite our instinctive rebellion against silence, it is important that we sit in silence at least a few minutes a day. Why? Our unique wisdom lies within each present moment. There is always a lesson or insight to be drawn from our simple daily experiences. We only ever experience life in this moment. The future doesn't exist. It only shows up as the present. The only way to connect with these insights is to be quiet.

Silence is the medium of communication between us and our Spirit. In silence, we receive inspiration. In silence, we begin to understand things we didn't understand before. We gain clarity. A few moments of silence every day clear our mind of the clutter that has gathered throughout the day. The clutter comes from the noise of the society in which we live. The noise comes from books, magazines, movies, TV, the Internet, co-workers, family, friends—the list goes on.

Remember, these sources don't necessarily provide bad information. But we must take some time to look at what we've accumulated to decide for ourselves if we want to get rid of anything. We often need to step away from the source of the information to understand it clearly. We need silence to see clearly. We need silence to see cleanly.

A few moments of silence every day clear our mind of the clutter that has gathered throughout the day. The clutter comes from the noise of the society in which we live. We need silence to see clearly.

We each see life through our individual filters. To some people who grew up financially poor, rich people are bad. So the people from the poor background reject Financial Wealth, consciously or unconsciously, from their lives. Some extremely talented and able women in corporations believe that the chief executive officer position is not a career possibility for them, so they never entertain the idea of going after that top job.

These filters are built from the conditioning we receive from our unique life experiences and the experiences of people around us. We often don't even realize that the filter exists. But two people with different filters take away different insights from the exact same experience. Let's say two people got fired from their respective jobs. One of them may see this as a great opportunity to go out and get a better job or start their own business. The other person may see this as the worst day of their life and never truly get out of the depression.

When we are living day-to-day, we often don't realize what may be driving our thoughts, and therefore, our actions. In clear thinking, silence enables us to see what filters we may have in place. If we know what filters we have, we then begin to make conscious decisions. Most of us react to life situations unconsciously by letting our filters decide for us. We may make right or wrong decisions. Being consciously aware of our filters is tremendously powerful. Silence enables us to step away from them, like an observer, and watch our filters at work. So if we choose, we can override a decision made by our filter. That is the power of silence.

We've all heard the common refrain: "Let me sleep on it." We hear some people say this before they make a major decision. Sleep is a tool that brings silence. It enables us to give the questions we have to that silent part of us, our Spirit, to help us decide. We can go on for days making long lists of pros and cons before we make a decision, but we never know everything there is to know. There is always an element of uncertainty. Our rational brain thinks in a logical and sequential fashion. Our Spirit knows without any rational analysis. To stay in connection with that Spirit, we must quiet the mind regularly. Then our Spirit can deliver its answer to us in the form of a gut feeling or intuition. Silence is a necessity for this.

Silence is both physical and mental. Physical silence is sitting still or lying down—that is, no physical exertion. Mental silence means listening to the silence of this present moment with no thoughts of the past or of the future.

It is not that difficult to be physically silent, although some of us do find this a little challenging. The more difficult part is mental silence. Thoughts race through our minds every second. But if we want silence, we can't resist these thoughts. Strangely, if we want to be silent and present in this moment, we just need to watch these thoughts as they connect with each other. One thought leads to another that leads to another—and the chain continues. All we need to do is become a watcher of our thoughts. That is all the effort needed in mental silence. This is all we need to do to be silent: Do nothing.

We can sit or lie down for a few minutes a day—there is no rule as to the length of time—and watch what is going on in our minds. By watching our thoughts, we begin to notice our filters. This may sound simple but it is very difficult to do. We inevitably lose track of our position as an observer and become one with a thought. We join the thought. Of course, we can't observe the beauty of a train if we are on that very train. We must stand in the fields outside to appreciate the sleekness of the train as it goes by. Each time we notice that we've joined a thought, and it will happen often, we don't need to get frustrated. We just need to start over and watch our next thought.

A great tool to hold our position as a casual observer is to write our thoughts down. Writing helps slow thoughts down so we can see them clearly on paper. Transferring our thoughts from the invisible mind onto a visible piece of paper reinforces our position as an observer.

After a while, we begin to have fewer thoughts. In between each thought, there is a gap of nothing but silence. The gaps contain space with no thoughts. This space could be as small as one second between two thoughts. All the wisdom we need to reach our full potential in life is found in this silent space. We must find a few minutes each day to watch the thoughts that inhabit our minds. In this way, we create this silent space. Then, we can visit this space and connect with its wisdom.

All we need to do is become a watcher of our thoughts. That is all the effort needed in mental silence. This is all we need to do to be silent: Do nothing.

We will be amazed by the experience. No movie or magazine or book (even this book, unfortunately) is more entertaining or insightful than the entertainment provided by our minds. But most of us never really bother to watch the never-ending movie that runs every waking moment in our minds. Just taking a few moments to watch our thoughts provides an immeasurable amount of wisdom. We may notice a pattern to our thoughts. For instance, our mind may instinctively focus on thoughts about the future, and its uncertainty may worry us. We may go over past occurrences or conversations and feel anger or resentment. We may think about a dream we have and feel excited about its potential for fruition. Either way, in silence, we begin to squeeze the wisdom out of our thoughts and emotions.

The silence we create is like a breath of fresh air. The wisdom we attract in our moments of silence soon begins to manifest itself in our daily lives. We become better able to be present fully in any moment during the day. Our ability to focus on something, anything, becomes stronger. Because it is so difficult to stand back and watch our own internal thoughts, practicing it makes it so much easier to focus on external things, such as following some other person's train of thought.

In conversation with people, we become better listeners. We listen with our entire being, not just with our ears. We listen to their words, but most importantly, we listen to the silence between the words: the pauses, the tone of voice, the inflections, and the energy from the speaker. We hear the verbal and non-verbal messages. We truly extract the wisdom from the interaction.

In a nutshell, in any activity, we develop the ability to concentrate better on what we're doing while we're doing it. We are able to eliminate the external and internal noise in order to completely immerse ourselves in what we're doing. Of course, if we do this, the outcome of the activity is much better. In my work, the time I spend not writing is probably more important than the time I do spend writing. My inactivity sharpens my insights. The benefits of sitting in silence show up in all areas of our life.

Another major reason why so many of us find it hard to do nothing is we associate physical activity, otherwise known as hard work, with success. I suffer from this affliction. With my achiever personality, I feel I need to accomplish something tangible every day. Many people are the same way. If we aren't doing something tangible, we call ourselves lazy, and, as most of us believe, success eludes the lazy one. We declare with complete certainty that the bum watching TV in his recliner every day will never amount to anything.

It is absolutely accurate that actions are required to bring success (whatever success means to each of us). But most of us waste too much energy in our actions. All action is not good action. All activity is not good activity. The clarity and wisdom from doing nothing (or sitting in silence) guide us to act only when necessary. There are situations in life when the best course of action is to do nothing. We don't have to be running constantly around the house or the office to achieve. There is no direct correlation between being busy and being successful.

So many of us also find it hard to do nothing because we associate physical activity, otherwise known as hard work, with success. All activity is not good activity. There is no direct correlation between being busy and being successful.

The modern workplace provides a great environment for the hyperactive busy body. At the office, most people assume that the worker who is always busy is obviously a valuable contributor to the team and therefore to the company. It is evident that he must be a hard worker. But physical exertion does not equal productivity.

On the other hand, there is another worker at the same office who never seems busy. In fact, he never seems to be hard at work. But somehow he gets just as much and sometimes more work done than his aforementioned busy colleague. This "lazy body" achieves the same amount of success by exerting less energy. Once again, the amount of physical energy we spend at work is absolutely irrelevant. What matters, what should matter, is the value we provide to others.

If we were the boss of these two workers and, due to financial constraints, we had to get rid of one of them, who would we let go of? Let's imagine this situation. If with focused concentration, the lazy worker can complete a task in one hour, and the busy worker running around all day completes the same task in a full eight-hour workday, we should be concerned. The lazy worker may not be challenged enough. The busy worker may be poorly organized. I'm not sure which worker we should keep on the team, but at the end of the day, we expect results.

Too many people confuse intense physical activity with productivity. As in our example, the busy worker may be poorly organized, so it takes him longer to get his tools in place to get his job done. Or he may have poor concentration skills and is not able to focus completely on the task at hand, so he is easily distracted and runs around, which prolongs the length of his projects. Or, he may have poor timing. He may be exerting himself when it is unnecessary and relaxing when it is necessary to apply himself fully to get the best results. After all, no one can sustain the exact same level of physical intensity forever. We inevitably go into periods where our intensity diminishes.

The benefits of sitting in silence and of doing nothing are that these sharpen our faculty of concentration and our timing. We are able to be fully present in each moment. We extract wisdom from the present moment. So when we do act, our actions are inspired by our Spirit. They are not simply surface actions. They are not simply physical actions performed by our physical bodies. We connect with our Spirit, which guides our actions. We bring our Spirit into our actions as well, acting with our entire being—mind, body and Spirit. Our Spirit guides us and leads us to act only when our actions will produce the best results. If we are not inspired, then we should do nothing.

Each of us has a limited amount of energy in any given day, which we replenish through sleep. By only acting when inspired, we don't waste any energy. We don't run if we can walk. But when it's time to act, when the time is right, we focus every ounce of our being on the activity at hand. As such, we are able to perform at our maximum potential during the period of time, brief or prolonged, that we physically act. Inevitably, a focused mind produces positive results in less time than an unfocused mind.

The uninspired busy person wastes important energy on unimportant tasks. And when the big moment presents itself, he doesn't have a full energy tank available to support him. By spreading his energy around carelessly, he doesn't have the same laser focus as an inspired counterpart. The busy person may seem busy all the time, but he is far from productive. And understandably, he is not as successful in his endeavors as he could be.

Doing nothing sharpens our faculty of concentration and our timing. When we do act, we don't waste any energy and our actions are inspired. When it's time to act, we focus every ounce of our being on the activity at hand.

Our connection with our Spirit tells us, in each moment, when real action is needed. It is wise to do nothing but think quietly for seven hours and act with our entire being in the eighth hour. But most people keep doing stuff for the full eight hours, in the name of looking busy, with no clear understanding of what or when specific activities are truly important.

Not all our activities carry the same importance. For the specific outcome we'd like to produce, some of the activities on our to-do lists are not as vital as others. Because some people never sit down in silence with themselves or look clearly at their daily tasks, they have lists of activities that will never lead them to their desired outcomes. Silence brings this clarity.

For instance, many people desire Financial Wealth. But they stay in employment situations with low fixed salaries, small incremental raises, and no potential for significant financial upside. No amount of running around every day at this job will bring the Financial Wealth they seek. They must move on to a different situation in order to give themselves a chance to live their dream. Being the most hard-working person in the current situation will not change the circumstances. In this case, their list of daily activities is inconsequential.

This fact seems obvious, but most of us don't see this clearly in our own lives. It is easy to stand back and point things out in someone else's life. But just like watching our thoughts, it is difficult to be a casual observer of our own lives. In our lives, we don't see things that clearly. Our filters distort the truth.

Just as it is important to be aware of what activities we perform, it is vital to know when we need to perform them. Some things are more important than others at a specific time. In order to manifest certain outcomes, sometimes we have a window in which we must act, otherwise we miss out on the big rewards.

This window is not necessarily an external window of opportunity. It is that internal nudge that we get from our Spirit that tells us that this moment is the time to act. This is when our undivided attention and intense energy is compulsory. In this moment, we can't afford any distractions. When we get that nudge, we must bring all our resources together in our actions. Every fiber in our being is needed right then and there.

Most people spend at least eight hours at work each day. Does this mean that each moment of those eight hours is a productive moment? Absolutely not. Some of these moments are spent expending valuable energy on trivial tasks, tasks that don't contribute positively to desired outcomes.

Do we need to run around the office? Would we lose any valuable time if we walked instead? Is the attention we pay to petty office gossip or turf wars the best use of our time and energy? Do we need to get worked up because the photocopy machine broke down again? Too many of us waste too much energy on things just like these. The inspired person understands that he has limited energy in his tank, and he uses as little energy as possible on these unimportant tasks. He conserves his energy for the big moments when his Spirit nudges him to action.

When we sit in silence, when we do nothing, we begin to see what is truly important and when. In this way, we are able to achieve more by spending less energy. Hard work does not equal success. I know we've heard a million times, "Work hard." Firstly, if we are working at a passion, it is never work. Work is play. Secondly, it's just not the best advice to give or receive. Change "Work hard" to "Work smart."

Believe me, hard work is common. It can be found in millions of workplaces all over the world. Tons of people work hard every day and get nowhere. Smart work is the rare gem. Few people work smart. Few people sit silently with these two questions: What am I doing? Why am I doing what I'm doing?

Most of us are running around so busy and hyperactive that we never stop to examine our activity. We never ask ourselves where we are running to and why, or whether the way we currently spend our time will even get us to where we want to be. These are simple and obvious questions. But most of us find it difficult to sit silently long enough for our Spirit to provide the answers to us.

If we find time to sit in silence, our insights become clearer. We see the reasons for our actions. Then, we slowly begin to understand which actions are important and when they are important. Soon, our actions become more inspired and thus have more impact. We waste little to no energy on activity for activity's sake. This is the power of sitting in silence alone with ourselves: our choice of activity is more discriminatory and more powerful.

If we find time to sit in silence, our insights become clearer. We slowly begin to understand which actions are important and when they are important. Our choice of activity is more discriminatory and more powerful.

While it is difficult to sit silently alone with ourselves, we must do it regularly. We will be in awe of the wisdom hidden within us in this very moment. We must connect with that wisdom. Our thought patterns in each moment shape our lives. We should try to learn what we think about regularly and why. By being aware of our pattern, which is determined by our filters, we can change what we don't like and keep what we do like. The interesting fact here is it requires little physical effort. Awareness of a thought is all we need to strengthen or weaken that thought. Awareness of self is the key to our success, whatever our definition of success is.

As we watch our inner movie, let's take note of the emotions that we associate with different thoughts. Emotions play a vital role in this process. They are here to guide us. If we feel unhappy, it simply means we are blocking the flow of Spiritual Wealth through us. Once we are aware of this, we can remove this block. The message from a negative emotion is just as important as the message from a positive one. The power of any negative emotion such as fear, anger, or worry is that we never take the time to be silent and look the negative emotion in the eyes. Just observing the thought or emotion renders it more and more powerless.

No one, besides ourselves, can know what is right for us in every situation. All the wisdom we need is found here in this moment. To connect with this wisdom, we need to be silent. Silence is the only medium of communication between us and our Spirit.

Let's get comfortable and be silent. Let's watch our thoughts and the silence between our thoughts. Then a whole new world of wisdom and beauty that has always been there begins to open up for us.

So go ahead, close this book, and try it out.

(I can't believe I just told you to close this book. But I'm sure we'll talk again soon.)

8. WHY DO WE PURSUE SIGNIFICANCE?

As far back as our childhood, we have felt a powerful urge to be part of the so-called "cool crowd." We want to fit in somewhere that matters. We want to be part of the group that people in our immediate circle consider significant.

As young children in school, most of us attempt to join the cool crowd, the sports jocks, the cheerleaders, or whichever group on campus receives the most attention and admiration. And if we can't become a member of that group, we sit on the outside and watch them with longing, hoping that, one day, they might invite us to join them.

Upon graduation from high school, we pray that some respected Ivy League establishment will accept us and allow us to study under its prestigious banner. As university students, we want to be invited to all the cool campus parties, join the popular clubs, and prove that we fit in by doing whatever everyone else is doing.

Upon graduation from university, we are advised by friends and family to choose a respectable career with strong earning potential. In our social lives, as adults, we line up for blocks outside the new trendy bar or club waiting to be allowed into the building by some heavyset security guard. Or, we do our best to secure a reservation at the hottest restaurant in town.

This is the pursuit of significance. It shows up in every area and stage in life. In adulthood, many of us settle into that respectable career, we buy a home in the right neighborhood, wear the right clothes, and drive the right car. We want our friends and neighbors to know that we are accomplished people as well. The only way for them to witness our accomplishments is if they recognize and respect our tangible and intangible achievements. Therefore, we ensure that our lifestyle conveys this message loud and clear to everyone we encounter: we fit in, we are significant. This is a very natural part of human nature. There is nothing inherently right or wrong with it. It just is what it is.

The pursuit of significance is the engine that drives so many of our decisions and actions in the world. We want to be regarded as important. We want to be perceived as significant. Remember this: we are eternally significant. We each have been blessed with unique and significant gifts that we are expected to share with the world. Every single one of us walking the face of the earth has this ability, this power. Deep down in our subconscious, we know that we are bigger than our simple physical circumstances. However, due to the conditioning we've received from our life experiences, we often lose sight of our innate power and settle on being like everyone else. This need to display our internal significance remains within us, and it presents itself in our actions, right or wrong.

There is no way for us to place our unique and eternally significant Spirit physically on a platter to present to the world. So we attempt to display our significance to the physical world by how we spend our time and money. We do and acquire things that clearly state our importance to all those watching, whether they are friends or strangers.

There is no way for us to place our eternally significant Spirit physically on a platter to present to the world. So we attempt to display our significance to the physical world by how we spend our time and our money.

If everyone in our social circle patronizes certain shops, restaurants, bars, or clubs, then that is exactly where we want to be seen. We want to go where the people we consider important go. We want to sit with these important people. Our association with these people makes us feel important. Rubbing shoulders with this group of people makes us feel taller.

Each of us has a definition of what we view as important. In school, during lunchtime, young people often sit in groups at tables based on what they view as the important table. If a child cannot get access to the important table of her choice, then she's relegated to a less important one. The same concept applies in adulthood. We want to be at the same restaurants as the important people. We want to sit at the same table with them. We want to reserve the most important table at the restaurant. From childhood to adulthood, the biological age changes, but the underlying need for significance is the same.

Luxury goods businesses understand this need and sell significance in every product that they offer. The message is a simple one: If we buy their product, we gain instant significance. Buy the product and join the people who matter. All the luxury items in categories such as cars, clothes, houses, art, or yachts that we see everywhere carry this message. The product tells the world that its owner is significant. Luxury products are the ideal tool to convey to others that we are in the right career or income bracket, especially if our audience immediately recognizes the product. The product states that we are somewhere important in life and that we are evidently going places.

Other purchases, such as a particular T-shirt, can tell our friends that we are a proud member of the trendy set. We always need to feel like we are part of a group. This is one of the reasons groups of friends, men or women, often dress in a similar fashion. We can even test this theory by watching our own friends, and we will notice that many people in our social circle dress similarly.

This pursuit of significance doesn't only show up in the products that we purchase. It is also evident in the type of people with whom we choose to spend time. We like to spend time with people who share our passions and ambitions. We like to associate with people whom we admire and would like to model. Sometimes, we feel the need to join certain clubs or organizations. If every executive at our company has a membership to the country club and we are either an executive or have ambitions to become an executive, we feel we need to join that club.

Outside the business arena, two areas that have conventionally never been considered ways to attract significance—philanthropy and spirituality—are slowly being infused with the cachet of significance.

Some people promote their involvement in charitable work in order to be applauded and recognized for it. In some cases, philanthropy has become an invaluable tool to boost a professional career. The charity event has become the ideal medium to network with people who can push a career forward. Charitable donors can garner the respect and admiration of their peers. Please don't get me wrong—a lot of philanthropic projects are undertaken for the pure joy of giving. But some projects are launched in order to bring significance to the event organizers and donors.

In the arts, some artists consider it a badge of honor to be viewed by their peers as spiritual. Their opinions on spirituality or their evident search for spiritual growth attract the admiration of their peers. In their world, spirituality brings significance.

These are some of the ways that we use our time and money to prove our importance to the world. In a way, by doing these things, by pursuing significance, we seek a certain level of fame, whether this fame is on a small or large scale. In essence, the pursuit of significance truly is the pursuit of fame. For a brief moment, or maybe even for an extended period, we want the world to pay attention to us. Some of us long for prolonged periods in which the world constantly recognizes our significance. This extended recognition is what we call "celebrity."

This powerful need for recognition drives our obsession with the culture of celebrity today. Deep down inside, none of us wants to be average. None of us wants to disappear in a crowd of people. So we admire people who seem not to be average. We admire the celebrity who doesn't have to sell the world on his or her significance. The world already knows it. Like that significant person, we want to distinguish ourselves from the crowd.

> **In essence, the pursuit of significance truly is the pursuit of fame. For a moment, we want the world to pay attention to us. Deep down inside, none of us wants to be average.**

The irony is that, although we want to stand out from the crowd, we also don't want to be left behind by the crowd. We want to stand out, but we don't want to stand out too much. This is why we do what the important people in our crowd do. We go to the same places, buy the same products, speak the same language, and wear the same clothes as the crowd that we consider important. We don't want to be average, but we do what members of our crowd do. As such, we inevitably do become average. This even applies to people we may instinctively think of as separate from the crowd, such as the people we consider celebrities and rebels. So many celebrities do what all the other celebrities around them are doing, so they become the average celebrity. In the same way, a crowd of rebels is still a bunch of people who look and act the same.

It is risky to distinguish ourselves too much from the crowd. We may become outcasts who have to travel alone. We may not fit in with any group of people. We may not be allowed into the important places. We may be viewed as weird and eccentric. In a nutshell, we may not attract significance. Because of this, human beings seek significance and distinct recognition from the crowd by being part of that same crowd. I know, it sounds strange, but this is the complexity of human nature.

> **Human beings seek distinct recognition from the crowd by being part of that same crowd. This is the complexity of human nature.**

Over the ages, businesses have recognized the instinctive herd mentality of human beings. Business understands that people buy what others are buying and do what others are doing. People are attracted to the bar or club that has a long line of other people waiting outside it. So, the bar or club staff make their patrons wait outside a little longer than necessary. People covet the restaurant where it is the most difficult to get a reservation. A fully reserved restaurant implies that other people want to eat there, so it has to be a good restaurant. Once again, the restaurant staff makes it a little harder to get a good reservation. It creates the perception that it is a place where everyone wants to be, so of course, we should want to be there as well.

In financial investing, it is easier for a financial advisor to sell her clients on stocks that everyone else is buying than it is to convince a client to buy a stock that few people own. Everyone loves the new hot stock that has a price that is rising every day, because everyone else is buying it. No one wants to be left out of potentially huge profits. In the retail business, people are attracted to the store that already has a crowd inside its doors.

In each of these business examples, people assume that if there is already a crowd somewhere, there must be something significant there. As P.T. Barnum, the famous pioneer of the modern circus, once said, "Nothing draws a crowd like a crowd."

What happens to the courageous few who do step away from the crowd? These people are either given the label "genius" or "crazy." These are the two potential extremes where these loners have to live.

Being labeled "crazy" means that we probably don't attract significance. We are ignored. Being different is difficult. But remember, we are not talking about being different for the sake of being different. We are talking about being our true selves. We do what feels right to us regardless of what everyone else is doing. We go where we want to go, even if it's not the trendy place. We have to walk alone a lot of the time.

Most people walk down paths in their personal and professional lives that have been carved out by millions of people before them. There is an existing model to follow. They just have to do what has been done before, and everything will be okay. They walk with the crowd.

Walking alone means that we can't hide behind a wall of people. We are naked. All our flaws and eccentricities are visible for the world to see. If we dress differently, work in unconventional careers, drive a peculiar car, or speak differently, we separate ourselves from the crowd. The crowd, friends or strangers, may peg us as weird or crazy. We may not get invited to the parties with all the cool people.

Because of the possibility of this situation, most of us sit comfortably in between the genius and the crazy person—we sit in the middle with the crowd. We don't dare to stray too far out of the fold. We want respect within the crowd. Staying with the crowd brings significance.

The other extreme is that we are recognized as a genius—a visionary who doesn't follow trends but creates them. The world follows our lead. We are being ourselves, expressing our Spirit in our personal and professional lives, and people watching us decide that they like what they see and adopt our vision and actions.

This is the significance that most of us truly want, but the journey to the destination called "genius" often runs through the city called "crazy." There's no guarantee that the world would finally come to recognize our genius. We may never reach that destination called "genius."

We are walking down a road that hasn't been clearly laid out by anyone before us. We have to live with the fact that we may often get lost. Uncertainty and insecurity are constant companions on our journey. Even worse, because people would rather follow the crowd than the lone wolf, loneliness is another demon with which we have to deal. The world may always view us as crazy, weird or eccentric. As such, most people would rather not embark on such a trip.

We often believe it is safer to be part of the crowd. It is safer to follow the accepted trends. It is safer to live like everybody else. But we all have a genius within. We have unique gifts that no one walking the earth has. The genius follows his own Spirit irrespective of whether the world catches on or not. If we are lucky, the world may recognize our genius. This recognition of our genius brings significance.

The courageous few who do step away from the crowd are either given the label "genius" or "crazy." The journey to the destination called "genius" often runs through the city called "crazy."

The purpose of this conversation is not to judge our thoughts or actions, but to wake up and observe them. It is important for us to be conscious of why we do what we do. Our need for significance is not a bad thing. There's absolutely nothing wrong with seeking significance by doing certain things or by purchasing certain items. Significance is a natural human motivation. Remember, once again, we are each born significant. Regardless of our physical circumstances, whether we are homeless or live in mansions, we are eternally significant. We have been blessed with freedom of choice, so we get to choose for ourselves what we want and don't want in our lives.

The intention here is for each of us to observe the pursuit of significance as it plays out in our daily lives. The questions that arise within us regarding significance and the positive or negative emotions that accompany these questions will lead to our own individual answers.

There is no reason to resist seeking significance. True power lies in being aware of what we're doing, when we're doing it. The power lies in waking up to our actions, so that if we decide to seek significance by doing something, we are doing it consciously. If we decide not to do it, this is a conscious choice, too. All we need to do is observe what we're doing when we're doing it.

Would I eat at this restaurant if no one were watching? Would I buy this car or these clothes if no one ever got to see them? Would I buy this house if I never got to show it off to anyone? Would I frequent this bar if it wasn't considered the trendy place to be? Would I buy this stock if no one else were buying it? Would I join this country club if it provided no boost to my career or my image? Asking ourselves questions like these opens us up to self-exploration. Let's see where our questions lead us.

We are each born significant. Regardless of our physical circumstances, whether we are homeless or live in mansions, we are eternally significant.

---

9. IS MY TRUTH YOUR TRUTH?

I'll tell you up front: My truth is not your truth. Your truth is not my truth.

What is true for me may not be true for you. What is right for you may not be right for me. What may work for me may not work for you. So then why do people write books instructing us on what we should do? In this specific case, why would I write this book if I think my ideas may not be true for you? I write to share my questions and my truth with you, so that you can explore your questions and discover your truth. I write to trigger questions in you.

It is also important to note that the process of searching for answers, for truth, is more important than the answers that we may uncover. In fact, the uncertainty that our questions bring is where the real wisdom lies. The real power is in not knowing, and therefore, exploring. The power is in the journey of self-exploration, not in settling on a conclusive answer to each question that arises. As I mentioned at the beginning of this journey, the wealth is in the questions, not in the answers.

We must explore each moment of life. Each moment must be examined with fresh eyes. Past experiences provide a reservoir of knowledge to draw from and thus can help us come to quicker decisions in our personal and professional lives. But experience can sometimes be a significant weakness. It could cloud our judgment, since we may carry preconceived notions with us and we can't see this new moment clearly.

The objective here is to nurture the process that we use to find our own answers. Our truth comes from our unique Spirit. We need to develop a stronger connection to our Spirit that guides us wisely, moment to moment.

The process of searching for answers, for truth, is more important than the answers that we may uncover. The wealth is in the questions, not the answers.

The journey of self-exploration never ends. When we get into a car, we know where we want to end up, and we get out of the car once we reach that destination. But self-exploration is a peculiar journey. There is no destination. We never get "there." No two moments in our life are ever identical. Every moment is unique. Every moment holds new wisdom. We must observe each moment with clean eyes. We must become young again in each new moment. We never stop learning. That is the power that youthful innocence often has over experience.

By the way, youth and innocence has nothing to do with biological age. The youth and innocence that I allude to is the youth of the Spirit. There are biologically young people who are truly old people in spiritual terms. These biologically young ones form rigid opinions on different life matters and impose their beliefs on the beautiful new experiences that they encounter throughout their lives. These so-called young people are, in fact, old. They no longer see what really is. Their beliefs, developed from their own experiences, what they have observed, and what they have been taught, cloud their vision. They are spiritually old because their Spirit, which is eternally young, is being suppressed.

On the other hand, there are biologically older people who have tons of experience but are still open to learning from each new moment. They see the never-ending beauty and wisdom in the world every day. They explore the lessons that each new simple daily encounter brings. They can still smile and laugh wholeheartedly in the midst of all that they do not know. They embrace their uncertainty about life. They embrace the mystery of life. They enjoy the never-ending process of searching for answers to life's questions. Regardless of how old these people are in biological terms, they are young and innocent in Spirit.

Once again, my truth is not your truth. And your truth is not my truth. But in our society, we constantly try to transfer one person's truth to the next person. If someone somewhere is successful at something, we assume that all we must do is list out exactly what they did and do it, too. We will then be able to achieve the same thing. We often forget that the successful person was created with his own unique Spirit.

Science may be able to clone the human body. But no amount of advanced scientific technology will ever succeed in replicating a human Spirit. Furthermore, science can never create in another person all the exact same life experiences and circumstances that the successful individual lived in her life. Her unique experiences and circumstances play integral roles in her success story. Each of us is born with a unique Spirit. Our Spirit holds our gifts, our eccentricities, and the things that make us each special. But most of us run away from our uniqueness. Instead, we choose to adopt the traits of some other person. We try to adopt their truth because they are successful. But it is not our truth.

Our unique Spirit holds our unique truth. Science may be able to clone the human body. But no amount of advanced scientific technology will ever succeed in replicating a human Spirit.

Of course, I'm not implying that we shouldn't study the path and principles of people who are successful in our chosen field. It's important to learn from those who went ahead of us. As the saying goes, "We can see further if we stand on the shoulders of giants." It makes our journey a little easier since we can use their knowledge to move us forward faster. A lot of successful people write books or tell their stories on television, in newspapers or magazines. If we are lucky, we get to meet our idols in person and have conversations with them.

So there is no need to reinvent the wheel if someone has already written the playbook. However, we must remember that there is always more to their success than any playbook can cover. The successful individual has unique traits, gifts, and experiences that we will never be able to replicate. Even if we follow their playbook word for word, day after day, we will never be that person.

This may sound pessimistic but it is actually far from it. It is the most powerful and beautiful piece of information we can ever have. It means that we will never be a carbon copy of someone else. We can be our own great self. We admire that successful individual because she is being herself. We simply have to do the same.

Our great self may even achieve, in material terms, much more than the teacher who taught us. In spiritual terms, there is no competition or comparison between any two people. We each reach our maximum potential. We can study what those before us have learned, add our unique Spirit to the playbook, and reach our own maximum potential.

Unfortunately, our society teaches the opposite of this. Our media outlets tell us that we need to be like the people they profile. They say that if we want to be successful, we must do exactly as these people have done. This attitude of society will never change, so it's our individual responsibility to look at the information we are fed and decide what is right for us.

In fact, sometimes the principles used by that successful individual are completely wrong for us. Remember, your truth is not my truth. Because someone else has achieved something significant, it does not mean their process is right for us. Their truth may be totally inappropriate for us. We must explore our Spirit to find out if it feels right. If it's not right, it's not right.

It doesn't matter who the teacher is. If Bill Gates, one of the world's richest people, gives us advice on how to build huge Financial Wealth, let's listen and take notes, but we must question whether his methods are also right for us. Gates has specific unique gifts and unique experiences that have led him to build his Financial Wealth. We each have our own unique gifts. Not all of his advice may be applied successfully to our specific situation.

In everyday human interactions, people are quick to tell others what they should be doing. One of the most common needs for us as human beings is our need to be proven right. I'm sure we have all witnessed situations in which someone would fight to the death to make sure his point of view is deemed the correct one. During the fight, in the heat of emotion, he's no longer interested in any other possibly legitimate opposing views. He has decided that he is right, and he is simply waiting for his opponents to agree with him. Logical reason no longer has a place at the table. We describe someone like this as having strong opinions, or as being strong-willed.

If we are honest with ourselves, we will admit that this individual is often that familiar face looking back at us in the mirror every morning. We each love to believe that we are right, that our truth is the only truth.

Millions of hours of programming on television are built around this premise. We have business shows where journalists, analysts, and experts converge to give their opinions on past events or make predictions on where business and financial markets are headed. A similar approach is used on political or religious shows, two areas in which people express some of their strongest beliefs. Those involved in these debates present their opinions—their notion of the truth. The debates get heated as each side seeks the validation that their point of view is correct and that the other side is wrong.

Every week, these debates go on. Do we really believe that, in a brief debate, we can go into someone's mind and replace all the past conditioning that has led to their beliefs with our new ideas? Absolutely not. We agree to disagree in order for the show not to go on forever, and we close the debate. The show's viewers benefit from different perspectives. The debaters are given a podium to express their beliefs. Finally, we each have to decide for ourselves what we believe.

We each love to believe that we are right, that our truth is the only truth.

In our personal lives, we often judge people based on what we deem is right or wrong. We may judge the character trait or action of a friend. We are quick to jump to conclusions if we think that the action or trait is inappropriate. In an interesting way, it makes us feel good to know that we are right and the friend is wrong. It gives us a sense of superiority. We feel like we are a more intelligent or better human being than the other person. We seek the validation of our superior intelligence by giving advice to, confronting, or judging others. We may confront or give advice to the person openly. Or, we may simply judge him or her internally.

Each of us has lived through different realities. No two life experiences are ever the same. Even siblings, who grow up in the same household, emerge with different belief systems about themselves as individuals and about the world as a whole. The experiences and the unique Spirit shape the individual and lead to the character traits or actions that we see. Unless we have lived that individual's life and have their unique Spirit, we will never understand the entire reason behind their traits or actions. We will never completely understand their truth. So please, let's try not to judge.

One of the strongest urges we feel is the urge to give advice, to tell the other person not to be that way or do what they do. We want to transfer our truth to that other person. We want the other person to agree with our remarkably intelligent advice and to immediately change their behavior. This will not happen.

Belief systems are deeply ingrained in a person's being. Even professionally trained psychiatrists find it difficult to change people's belief systems. They are not altered after a fifteen-minute conversation or debate. We may be absolutely right in our intelligent remarks. But people change when they are ready to change, not when we decide we want them to change. Our beautifully eloquent arguments make relatively no difference.

Let the other person live his own life. Let his process unfold as it should. Each of us follows a unique path in life, with simple daily experiences that carry tremendous wisdom in them, so let the individual learn from his own experiences. The reason we have different experiences is so we can each receive our lessons in our own time.

Our remarks to the other person may sometimes spark the process of self-exploration in that person. But more often than not, people identify so much with their beliefs that our advice may do more harm than good. By giving advice, we may cause their beliefs to become stronger as they defend them with increased intensity. Let's not force our thoughts down anyone's throat. Some polite people may actually listen to our advice but resent us afterwards for questioning or attacking their beliefs and their intelligence. Let people learn in their own time. Unless the other person is in a life-threatening situation, let's keep our mouths shut.

Unless we have lived the other's life and have their unique Spirit, we will never completely understand their truth. So please, let's try not to judge.

It is relatively easy to keep our mouths shut but it is much more difficult to be non-judgmental, which is an internal process. Judgment of others feeds our ego. It makes us feel like we are better than the person that we judge. We often automatically judge strangers that we see or meet. Sometimes we have a specific predetermined verdict for people who fit a specific label in our mind.

We may see a homeless man on the street and judge him as lazy or inferior to people who do have homes. We may see a man with a luxury car and expensive clothes and automatically judge him as rich and snobbish or smart and superior to us. In some cases, we judge people based on the beliefs we attach to different lines of work. If a woman reveals that she is an exotic dancer, most people immediately view her as repulsive, almost a second-class citizen. If another woman introduces herself as a medical doctor, we automatically decide that she is respectable and intelligent.

Most of us have a long list of labels and judgments attached to each of these labels. Once we label someone, we can no longer see the true Spirit of the person behind the label. We use labels to interact with people in our world. We meet someone, and we immediately want to form some opinion about them. Hence the most overused question in social interactions today: "What do you do for a living?" Within minutes of meeting someone, we ask this question. It helps our judgment process. From the response we get, we begin to decide what kind of person this other human being is. Is she respectable based on society's standards of respectability? Is she rich? Is he intelligent? Is he caring? The labels provide us with ready-made answers. We can now pass judgment.

The truth is that no label, job title, or even physical appearance can capture the entire unique Spirit of any one person. Our work or appearance may be an expression of who we are, but it is never the whole story.

The homeless man is not inferior to anyone. In fact, he can't be since he was created with his own unique gifts, just like the rest of us. The exotic dancer may be a warm and caring person, but simply makes her living in a line of work that is deemed unconventional by society. The rich man may be compassionate, not in the least snobbish, and not any more intelligent than the average man on the street. He may have simply found a way to share his unique Spiritual Wealth with the world and received Financial Wealth in exchange. The doctor may be intelligent in medical terms, but not very intelligent in other areas of life.

Everyone we encounter—friends, relatives, or strangers—has a story. Everyone has had life experiences that brought them to this moment. The only way we can know and understand the real person is to live that person's story. Because we can't do that, let's not rush to judge anybody.

We inevitably form first impressions when we meet people or simply walk past them. We can't and need not resist that instinctive reaction.

But let's remember that first impressions always provide an incomplete picture and are often totally inaccurate. We may not approve of the other person or what he or she is doing, but it may be right for him or her. Let them be. Let them live their own truth.

The most overused question in social interactions today is, "What do you do for a living?" But the truth is, no label can capture the entire unique Spirit of anyone.

As we mentioned earlier in this chapter, on our journey of self-exploration we must look at each new moment with young and innocent eyes. Therefore, we shouldn't attempt to transfer truth blindly from one experience to the next. Truth is not rigid. Truth doesn't stay the same every day, or even every moment. Each moment in life is unique and carries its own truth. We may have a similar experience today as we had in the past, but this doesn't mean that the answers that we uncovered in the past necessarily work for this situation today. Our past experience and knowledge is a great starting point for exploration, but ultimately, we must look at this new situation with fresh eyes.

If we have a new experience with new questions and automatically apply our past answers, we grow stale and old. We simply repeat the past. We lose our youth. We lose the ability to see the new. We're like a machine that has been fed information on what to do in specific situations, and it executes with no emotion, with no Spirit.

Every moment brings its own wisdom. If we can't see and live the moment, we can't see and live the wisdom. It's that simple. Too many of us act like machines. We are unaware of our conditioning from past experiences, so we react to new situations in the same unconscious way. We decide on the answer before we even listen to the question. We never bother to look at why we believe what we believe. We are basically asleep at the wheel of our lives. Our lives are on autopilot. We completely miss out on the beauty of the present moment. Truth lies in each moment. Truth is not transferred blindly from one experience to another.

Truth lies in each moment. Truth is not transferred blindly from one experience to another.

For instance, we may have read a book a while ago. The book contained certain insights that we absolutely soaked up instantly and other pieces of information that somehow didn't speak to us as intensely as the other insights. Then, for some reason, today we come back to the book, and suddenly we're fascinated by the information that we didn't quite appreciate before. In this new moment, it all makes sense. This moment is the right time for that formerly unappreciated information. The past moment was not. Today, we may find ourselves in a new place in life, so this wisdom, that was always there in front of us, that was incomprehensible or uninteresting in the past, now makes perfect sense. In this new moment, we get it.

We experience a similar scenario sometimes when we receive advice from parents. At earlier stages in our lives, we may simply not understand what our parents were trying to say. As children, we even find some of the advice boring or useless. Then, one day, later in life, we understand what our parents meant. That day, that moment, carries the wisdom. We discover the truth.

This once again reiterates why we can never force the truth on someone else, even as parents talking to children. The child will get it when he is supposed to get it—and not one second before that right moment. If the truth is not really the child's truth, he will never get it. He may try to adopt it because it was passed down to him by a parent or an authority figure, but it will never work for him. Each lesson has its time. And each person has his or her truth.

The timeless beauty of love is in the ability to accept the other person as they are, not as we want them to be. Love is about not trying to impose our truth on other people. Let others find their own truth. Let others live their own truth.

So, in conclusion, don't rush to judge or throw around your advice. You may be right. You may be wrong. Either way, it doesn't matter. I know you believe you're right. I do, too.

My truth is not your truth. Your truth is not my truth.

---

10. WHY DO WE FEAR UNCERTAINTY?

Webster's dictionary defines *uncertainty* as something that is "not definitely known." For instance, the outcome of some present or future event is unknown to us mortal beings. We can't predict it with absolute certainty. In other words, anything can happen—good or bad, success or failure.

Of course, whether something is good or bad depends on the particular person looking at the situation. What may be good to me may be bad to you. What may be considered a resounding success by one person may be a failure to another person.

In a game of singles tennis, at the end of the match, one player wins and one player loses. From the loser's perspective, this is an unwelcome outcome. From the winner's vantage point, the outcome is perfect. To a disinterested third party, the outcome is neither good nor bad. Same outcome, different perspectives.

The third party is like nature, which doesn't judge or label anything. In the rules of tennis, created by us humans, someone must win and someone must lose. But nature has no rules regarding this man-made game, and like the third party observer, it doesn't label this outcome a success or failure, good or bad, as we humans do. It doesn't matter what the outcome is. Life goes on.

Before we continue our conversation, the important point we need to establish here is that the words "good" and "bad," "success" and "failure," are man-made inventions to rate man-made games in life. These games and their rating systems have nothing to do with nature. In nature, nothing is good or bad, nothing is a success or a failure. It just is as it is.

The words "good" and "bad," "success" and "failure," are man-made inventions to rate man-made games. In nature, nothing is good or bad, nothing is a success or a failure. It just is as it is.

In these man-made games that we undertake in our personal or professional lives, we've established that there are two potential outcomes: good and bad. Therefore, we can assume that there's an equal chance of either one of these outcomes presenting itself. So then why is it that when we're faced with uncertainty, most of us tend to focus our thoughts on our definition of a bad outcome? Somehow our negative thoughts suppress our positive thoughts. The thoughts of what we don't want to happen bring fear. We fear the uncertain future.

Fear is an extremely strong emotion. We all feel fear sometimes. We don't know for sure what will happen if we attempt something, so our uncertainty brings the emotion of fear. Fear has come to be identified by society as a negative and unpleasant emotion.

Why do we call fear a negative emotion? Something negative is something we don't want in our lives. But fear is what causes a deer to bolt off running when it picks up the scent of a nearby lion. Fear saves its life. Fear is what causes us humans to jump out of the way of an oncoming vehicle if we believe it may run into us. Once again, fear saves lives. Fear is what has pushed society to build safety features into cars, planes, and all sorts of products. The fear of what could happen if we didn't have these safety devices produces these technological advances. These examples demonstrate the importance of fear in our lives. The heavy pounding of our hearts when we are in danger, the instinctive reactions by our bodies, caused by fear, save our lives. Fear is necessary. Fear, in this sense, is good.

On the other hand, fear can paralyze us. In the worst case scenario, the emotion of fear brought on by uncertainty can cause us not to attempt anything new. We become afraid that the outcome may be undesirable. Our fear becomes our master, it takes control of our beings, and we do as it says. We are each a Spirit bigger than any emotion. It is never good for an emotion to engulf us. In this case, fear is bad.

So is fear a positive or negative emotion? We have seen that it can be good and bad. But, at the same time, fear is neither good nor bad. Fear, in each of these cases, is like any other emotion—it carries a message. Each moment we experience in life holds our truth and our wisdom. In the moment that we feel fear, there is a message that the emotion brings with it. We have been given the freedom to listen to the message and the power to decide what we want to do. When we see a car hurtling towards us, we receive a message and jump out of the way of the vehicle. When we feel unhappy at a job and contemplate leaving it, the fear of the unknown presents itself. We have the freedom to decide whether we want to listen to that fear and stay put, or acknowledge but ignore the fear and move into the unknown.

Fear can save lives, and fear can paralyze. Like everything else in nature, fear is neither good nor bad. It carries a message. We have the freedom to listen to the message and the power to decide what we want to do.

Fear always attempts to protect us from possible dangers that the unknown future may or may not bring. But our fear doesn't know what will, in fact, happen in the future. Fear is a simple tool that gives us advanced warning, and thus forces us to examine our decisions closely. If fear didn't exist, we would jump out of a plane at 30,000 feet with no parachute, without thinking twice about it.

Fear plays an important role in life, but we are always bigger than our fear. We have the power to step back and decide whether the fear is justified in the specific situation. If it is, we listen to it. If it's not, we acknowledge the fear but move forward with our plans anyway. We never have to fight or suppress fear. Why would we fight with tools that we control? Why would a plumber fight with his tools? All we have to do is observe the tool, like a powerful master, every time it shows up in our lives.

Fear is an emotion created to work for us. However, we human beings created the word "fear" itself. We created the definition of the word. If we choose to, we can change our personal definition of fear from the current description calling it negative. Because we are each powerful masters, we can redefine our tools any way we want. Fear is not negative. Fear is not positive. Fear is simply an emotion that brings wisdom like any other emotion, such as love, hate, joy, or sorrow.

As we noted previously, if we feel no fear, then we might attempt to jump out of a plane without a parachute. The reason for this lack of fear could be that we are completely unaware of the consequences that this jump could bring. If we don't know about the danger involved, then we are basically confident and certain that we will be okay after our fall. Of course, the laws of nature would prove that our confidence is misplaced. The point to note here is that our certainty causes us not to fear. There is zero uncertainty, so there is zero fear. Certainty means that we are absolutely sure about something. We know with total confidence that if we undertake something, the outcome will be exactly as we predict.

Certainty is definitely not as exciting as uncertainty. Certainty can be boring, while uncertainty is exciting. But in nature, everything has its time and place. Nothing in nature is unnecessary. Boring is not bad. Certainty is not bad. Certainty has its place in life.

We are certain about gravity on Earth. We have established that if we throw an apple up in the air, it must fall back down to the ground. We know this with absolute certainty. As such, we have created things that take advantage of this certainty about gravity. We know that if we throw a ball up into the hoop on a basketball court, it will fall back down to the ground, so we can play the game of basketball. We are positive that a concrete sidewalk is hard enough for us to put our feet down when walking and not sink into the pavement like we would in a pool of water. We can then walk with certainty and not have to think about every single step we take on the sidewalk.

If we were uncertain about everything in life, we'd have to monitor every single action we took constantly. We'd go crazy. Certainty allows us to relax once we are certain about something. Then, we can focus on the uncertain things. However, we have to walk through the uncertain to become certain. We had to walk on the sidewalk to become certain that we would not sink into it. Once we are certain about the sidewalk, it becomes boring. We no longer have to focus on it, and we can refocus our thoughts and energy on more uncertain and exciting things.

Like certainty, uncertainty also has its time and place in life. Uncertainty keeps our minds working. It keeps us alive. We don't know what's coming, so we have to keep our eyes wide open. It forces us to stay young. It literally keeps our blood pumping faster. When uncertainty brings fear, our hearts pump blood faster throughout our body. We feel nervous. We feel excited. These are good emotions. They imply that we are living.

It is easy to settle into a comfort zone, a zone in which we are almost completely certain of the results of our actions. In this zone, our hearts may be pumping blood, but we are not living. We can perform activities in this zone with our eyes closed. We don't need to observe our actions through fresh, young, and innocent eyes. In a sense, our Spirit is dead. Every day above ground looks like yesterday. We look forward to nothing. This is why uncertainty is necessary. This is why we have uncertainty. It keeps us alive and kicking regardless of our age.

Certainty and uncertainty are both necessary in life. Certainty allows us to relax once we are certain about something. Uncertainty keeps us alive. We don't know what's coming, so we have to keep our eyes wide open.

The lesson here is that certainty and uncertainty are both necessary in life. They each play an important role. Let them be. Let's not label them negative or positive. Like day and night, we need them both. We face problems when we attempt to fight with or eliminate one or the other. We sometimes try to block the natural flow of certainty and uncertainty in our lives. When we take on any new challenge and it results in a defined outcome, it goes from the unknown to the known. We now know. Therefore, it moves from the realm of uncertainty to certainty. This frees up our time and energy so that we can explore more lands of uncertainty. This is a natural transition from uncertainty to certainty.

We attract heartache when we attempt to block this natural flow. The most common problem we face is when we try to stifle or eliminate uncertainty, when we want to be one hundred percent certain before we take on new challenges. But we will never achieve this level of certainty prior to actually undertaking a new venture.

As humans, we always seek the easiest way to do things. This is the primary reason why we are the animals with the most advanced tools and technology. Lions still chase down their prey. We stand still and shoot our targets with guns. In a similar fashion, in order not to face uncertainty, the easiest thing to do is simply not to try anything new.

But a Higher Power has intelligently given us emotions that will not allow us to live peacefully under these conditions. We feel bored, uninspired, and even depressed, when we live in our certain comfort zone. These emotions tug at our Spirit constantly. We know we need to wake up and live. If we fight the emotions and do nothing, they become more intense. We feel the constant energy drain from the lack of excitement in our lives.

Therefore, the uncertainty of the unknown must be allowed into our lives; otherwise, we'll never be happy. Life must flow freely between uncertainty and certainty. Of course, there are uncertain issues that we are not passionate about exploring, and we don't have to explore them if these issues are not of interest to us. But there will always be questions that excite us, questions to which we want answers. Life brings new questions every day. Uncertainty, at its core, is simply questions for which we don't yet have answers. Before we learned to drive a car, our ability to drive was a question. Once we learned to drive, we became certain that we could, and we moved on to the next question.

Life must flow freely between certainty and uncertainty. We have to walk through the uncertain to become certain.

We often feel that strong emotion called fear when we face uncertainty, and secretly, we love the feeling. We seek certainty, but subconsciously we truly love uncertainty. If we are certain about something, we don't need to explore it or learn anything new, since we know everything we need to know. Life becomes boring. We need excitement. We can't stop jumping off the proverbial cliff.

Uncertainty drives so many of our human creations. Uncertainty drives the stock market, gambling, the movie business, business startups, and so many other activities.

Once in a while stock markets crash, but Wall Street is still here. This is because investors believe that they can face the questions in the financial markets and find the right answers that will create profits.

In Las Vegas, everyone agrees that the house (casino) always wins. The odds are stacked in favor of the casino over the gambler. But the Las Vegas gambling industry is still thriving because we believe that we are lucky or smart enough to beat the house, at least sometimes. This uncertainty excites us. That excitement keeps the engine of the gambling industry going.

In Hollywood, movie producers and financiers know that the success of a movie is highly unpredictable. But movies are produced and financed regularly. The stakeholders take on the uncertain project with the belief that this movie will be successful. If it is successful, great. If it's not, they'll try again next time.

The venture capital industry follows a similar model. Most businesses that are financed by venture capitalists are failures. It is an accepted fact in the industry. But one overwhelming success could compensate for the dozens of past failures, so business ideas keep getting financed. The uncertainty keeps this industry humming along as well.

In a nutshell, we naturally fear uncertainty, but we secretly enjoy it. We go into an undertaking hoping for a specific outcome. The uncertainty keeps us awake. Our hearts beat faster. We are alive.

Whenever we enter the unknown, we bring something new into our lives, and therefore into the world. Innovation and creativity arise out of uncertainty. Every single creation in art, business, or science arises from uncertainty. Innovation comes from not knowing.

Every minor or major innovation begins with the question, "What if?" The new can be as simple as learning to drive a car. The skill was not here before, and now it is here. The fear of the unknown should be worshipped for its power to mine our Spirit for new ideas and new energy. Once we are certain about something, creativity comes to a halt. We no longer need to explore the question, "What if?" What we have accomplished is now certain, and we can focus our precious energy on more creative thoughts that lead to new creations.

The certain is known, is dead. The uncertain is unknown, is alive. Both life and death are natural transitions in existence. In the same way, the transition from uncertainty to certainty is natural.

The certain is known, is dead. The uncertain is unknown, is alive. Both life and death are natural transitions in existence. In the same way, the transition from uncertainty to certainty is natural.

We all know and accept the fact that we can't control the future. When we have a project that excites us and we decide to explore it, we generally hope to achieve a specific outcome. In order for this to happen, we attempt to stack the odds in our favor, and rightly so. Before we jump into the uncertain fray, we work hard to increase the probability that our desired outcome will manifest itself.

Before we go to play the basketball game, we practice. Before we take the exam, we study. Before we start the new business, we do some research. The fact that we choose to acknowledge and override any fear that we may feel is already tremendously powerful. We then prepare ourselves so that we are in a better position to succeed, based on our definition of success.

Whenever I have an important event coming up, like a presentation or business meeting, I am overly detailed, sometimes to a fault, about my preparation. I fuss over everything—every minor detail about my appearance, the words I will speak, my mannerisms, the physical room, you name it. This happens to me because my mind has a natural tendency to visualize how I want the event to unfold step-by-step. Before meetings, in my mind, I hear the words that the other party would speak to me. I also hear my insightful and witty responses to their comments.

Unfortunately for me, not even once have any of my mental visualizations ever played themselves out exactly in physical reality. The successful outcome that I envision is often achieved, but the path to get there is almost always significantly different from what I visualized before the event.

I know I never get it right in my mind, so why do I keep bothering with all the positive visualization and detailed preparation? I honestly can't stop the visualization. My mind always runs in that direction. It automatically creates images of what the place, people, or conversation will be like. I've learned over the years not to fight these images. I simply watch them in my mind like I would watch a movie. But the primary benefit of this visualization is it gives me confidence prior to the event. My overly intense preparation gives me the ability to tackle the unknown with poise. My confidence allows me to walk into the room, sit down, and let uncertainty take its place at the table.

The moral of the story is that uncertainty is an integral part of life. Let's simply observe the fear that uncertainty brings and decide consciously whether we want to stand still or move forward in spite of its presence. If we choose to enter the unknown, let's prepare ourselves properly, walk into the room, sit down, and let uncertainty take a seat, too.

Why fight uncertainty? Why fight the fear it may bring? Let it in. You and I know it will show up uninvited anyway. Let's not delude ourselves into believing that we can shut it out. The beauty of life is that, soon enough, uncertainty becomes certainty. Then we can move on to explore new uncertainty and exciting questions.

The beauty of life is that, soon enough, uncertainty becomes certainty. Let's invite them both into our lives today, tomorrow, and always.

11. WHAT DO WE REALLY HAVE TO LOSE?

The beauty of nature is timeless. There is no beginning or end date to nature's beauty. Time, of course, is a man-made creation that enables us to make plans and communicate with each other in one common language. We need to be able to decide when to do what. In other words, we need to know when our activities are scheduled to begin and to end, so we invented the days of the week, hours of the day, minutes of the hour, and seconds of the minute. We created the daily calendar and the clock in order that every human being works from the same reference point of time.

Time is a vital tool for us. It brings order to the potential chaos that would exist if each of us had our own individual definition of time in each moment of a day. Even before the advent of the clock, human beings used the positions of the moon and the sun in the sky as reference points to schedule activities with others. The concept of time facilitates this communication.

Nature knows nothing about time. It just goes on as it should. The timelessness of nature means that it is beyond this man-made concept called time. It is eternal. When we stand back and admire the ocean, flowers in a garden, animals in their habitat, or the sun setting in the horizon, we experience this eternal beauty. The sun doesn't check a clock to decide when it will rise or set.

There is no reason for the beauty of nature. There is no goal to it. In our lives, we always seek to comprehend the meaning of things, the reason why certain things happen. We always want to know where things will lead us. If we go to school, we hope to graduate and move on to the next phase of our lives. If we participate in sports, we hope to win at the game. If we go to work, we hope to achieve certain goals and receive a paycheck. Even as we read these words, we seek answers to questions or concerns we may have in our lives. This is human nature at work. We want and need to figure it out and get to it. Nature doesn't do this. It flows without searching for reason, without setting some destination in advance. There is no reason for the beauty of the ocean. We don't need to study it, we don't need to question it—we just need to live in it.

Moreover, no one owns nature. It is here for us all to enjoy. It belongs to all of us, and to none of us. The beauty of the sky, the sunset, animals, and the ocean are free to all of us. We don't need to offer any financial currency in order to experience it. It is free, unlike most material things in the world. We need money to purchase food, clothes, shelter, entertainment, and the long list of material things we enjoy in our modern world.

Just like time, money is another concept that we created out of basic necessity. Before the invention of money, people exchanged their goods for the goods of others. If I owned a horse and wanted to acquire a cow, and if they were each deemed of equal value, I could give my horse in exchange for the cow. Money places a financial value on my assets, such that if I have the accepted currency equal to the cow's value, I can offer my currency and receive the cow. I no longer need to trade my horse for the cow. Just like time, money facilitates this transaction. Once again, nature doesn't know the concept of money. Money means nothing to it.

No one truly owns anything in nature but in order to facilitate transactions, we have created products that define who owns what. In order to buy a house, we must offer money to the previous homeowner. Once this happens, we sign a document that gives us ownership of that house.

This concept of ownership, with or without a paper contract, is used in our monetary transactions, as ownership of items passes from one person to the next. It's only fair that the individuals who built the house be compensated for their work. They collected and combined materials from nature, such as soil and wood, to supply the building blocks of the house. In order for them to be rewarded for their work, money exchanges hands and the new homeowner is anointed. For utilitarian purposes, this is absolutely essential. Imagine if these rules of ownership didn't exist. Then anyone could walk into your home or seize something you own, and claim it as their own.

For utilitarian purposes, we created time, money and ownership of pieces of nature. But they are fictional. They mean absolutely nothing in nature.

In the material world, we have all agreed on these three essential concepts: time, money and ownership of pieces of nature. But the truth is, time and money are not real. They play no role in nature. In a similar fashion, the concept of ownership is fictional. We each own nothing. We came with nothing, and we will leave with nothing. We were born with no possessions, and we will die with no possessions. If we came with any belongings, then no one could take them away from us. It would therefore make sense that we must leave with them, but of course we don't.

We are spiritual beings who enjoy physical experiences. At birth, we bring our Spirit with us. Our Spirit holds the essence of who we are—our unique gifts and talents. We can never lose this Spirit because we don't own it. We are Spirit. We can't own what we are. Upon our death, our inheritors receive our material possessions, and even our physical bodies disintegrate and return to the Earth as dust. We don't take our bodies with us, but our Spirit lives on.

Most of us run away from the concept of death, but it is a necessary tool and a powerful motivator. Our mind, body and Spirit must flow in nature and move on elsewhere. Change is a natural part of life. The benefit of this knowledge is profound: If we know that we are a Spirit who came with nothing and we will leave with nothing regardless of how much material we accumulate throughout our lives, then we can lose nothing. There is absolutely nothing for us to fear because we have absolutely nothing to lose. How can we lose what we don't have?

The fears that we cultivate regarding losing our job, money, house, car, clothes, respect from peers, and the long list of other daily human worries are insignificant. When people come face to face with death, they wake up and realize that all that stuff really doesn't matter. The prospect of death brings this very simple concept to life. Then, after this experience, they truly choose to begin to live. Impending death is the ultimate wake-up call. The material possessions, the boring but lucrative job, the dreams of wealth, the beautiful plans for the future, and the recognition from peers no longer mean anything. These things are exposed for what they really are—irrelevant.

If we know that we are a Spirit who came with nothing and we will leave with nothing, then we can lose nothing. There is absolutely nothing to fear.

I don't advocate any theory that teaches repression of any kind. I believe in living consciously, observing our natural human tendencies, and pulling wisdom from our thoughts, emotions, and actions. As such, I will never encourage any of us to feel guilty about or renounce our material possessions. We don't need to repress, we just need to be aware of what we do when we are doing it.

Repression of anything simply gives that insignificant thing a higher level of significance. Running away from the house or car actually makes these ordinary pieces of wood and metal more powerful than they were before. We don't need to distance ourselves from anyone or anything. We just need to observe what we are doing and revisit our beliefs on the idea of losing something we own.

Personally, instead of the word "owner," I prefer the word "custodian." I remember watching a television interview with a renowned art collector who had acquired a large number of paintings by some of the world's most influential artists, such as Picasso and Monet. Initially, this collector had kept most of the masterpieces at his home for his private enjoyment. Then, he realized that, although he had paid a fortune for these works of art and therefore he was considered the owner, no one person truly owned the beauty of these paintings. It dawned on him he was not really the owner, he was the custodian. The paintings were currently in his possession for him to enjoy, nurture, share, and later, pass along. He immediately chose to display the pieces in a public museum for the world to enjoy as well.

Beauty, like nature, belongs to everyone and no one. No amount of money can buy beauty. For the purpose of transferring ownership, we set a price on the beauty of a painting, the view of a sunset from a penthouse apartment, the feel of the sand between our feet, and the sound of the waves at an oceanfront estate. We need this dollar value in order to operate according to the rules and conventions in our world. But, in reality, no amount of money can truly encompass the beauty we experience in the painting or the breathtaking view from the penthouse apartment and oceanfront property. If we purchase any of them, we become the custodians, not the owners. We don't own the view. It's for us all. We must share. We will eventually have to pass it on.

In fact, we derive immeasurable pleasure from sharing love and beauty with others. We often define philanthropy in terms of giving money to other people. As we discussed in the "What is Wealth?" chapter, money is one small part of true wealth. All wealth, including the Spiritual Wealth in love and beauty, can and should be shared. The art collector shared his love of the pieces he acquired with the world. The sound of the waves at the oceanfront property or the view of the sunset from the penthouse apartment brings us tremendous pleasure when we share it with loved ones.

A beautiful house is simply pieces of building material combined together. A beautiful home is the life, love and beauty of the people in a house. We can price the house, but we can never price the home. Once again, the paperwork may state that we own these material things, but we truly are custodians. The things are in our care, for now.

We are not owners of anything. We are custodians. Our stuff is in our possession for us to enjoy, nurture, share, and later, pass along.

Nature keeps moving along in an effortlessly wise and beautiful fashion, regardless of man-made creations such as time, money and ownership of things. This beauty and wisdom in flowers, the ocean, the sky, the rain, or the sun fascinate us. The wisdom and beauty that we enjoy on the outside in nature, we also have inside us, in our Spirit. Our Spirit is eternal, just like nature. We are part of nature. When we bring our Spirit into our work, we bring a piece of nature—our life—into our work.

Subconsciously, when working in Spirit, we are always trying to recreate the beauty that our Spirit observes in nature. We try to express our Spirit, our nature, in our work. This is why those who experience our work feel the timeless beauty and wisdom as they would feel in nature.

For instance, we feel the Spirit of the artist in the painting, the soul of the musician in the music, the passion of the businessman in his product, the grace and beauty of the athlete in her performance. We immerse ourselves in the experience, and it transports us into nature. We can put a price on the physical work, but we can never price its Spirit, passion, or beauty. The experience of nature in the work is priceless.

Savile Row is a small street in London that houses the shops of arguably some of the best men's tailors in the world. The work of crafting the male suit is an art form on this street. For decades, the most elegantly dressed men have commissioned custom suits from tailors on this legendary street. The older tailors on the street groom the younger tailors, who learn the delicate craft and take over after their mentors retire from the profession. The suits are so well-made that their owners almost always pass them on to their inheritors. A beautiful suit goes from a father to his son, from one generation to the next.

Savile Row doesn't follow fashion trends. It believes in timeless, classic style. Fashion trends come and go. But classic style never goes away regardless of the concept of time. In this line of work, we see how humans attempt to re-create the timeless beauty of nature. As the suit passes from father to son, it carries a story, heritage, and love in it that we can't price. We see the beauty of nature in a suit. The current owner of a Savile Row suit is merely its custodian. He enjoys the suit, cares for it, and eventually shares it with the next generation. This re-creation of nature in a suit, the timeless beauty, the love, the classic style are the primary reasons for the longevity of this small street in London dedicated to the fine art of men's style.

When we bring our Spirit into our work, we bring nature into our work. Those who experience our work feel the timeless beauty and wisdom as they would feel in nature.

In business, people seek ideas that enable a company to grow successfully today and keep its products around for a long time tomorrow. In other words, they seek the same longevity as in nature. Ironically, the ultimate marketing solutions are found in nature. Certain product manufacturers use nature for inspiration. Life and nature provide timeless wisdom.

The automaker Ferrari designs its luxury sports cars to mimic the beauty in the physical curves and grace of a woman. Salvatore Ferragamo, the women's shoemaker, studies the science of the human foot structure to design its shoes. The sounds in nature and life such as rain falling, ocean waves, thunder, or a heartbeat often inspire the most beautiful music. Ferrari's competitor, Lamborghini, designs its car engines to sound like music.

Our fascination with nature creates products that incorporate the most basic forms of nature, such as sunlight or water (the most cherished ones) in a penthouse apartment or oceanfront property. In our business world of impersonal email communication, a warm face-to-face connection with another human being is priceless. We see how, once again, the beauty of nature (the warm human being) is cherished. The human touch is timeless. No amount of marketing can replace the simple natural warmth in communicating with another human being.

The businessman may speak of owning his company. If we check the articles of incorporation or other ownership paperwork, he does. But spiritually, he doesn't. He is a custodian for the company. It is his responsibility to nurture the business wholeheartedly for all involved—the employees, customers, suppliers, and local community—to benefit from it and pass on an improved business to the next custodians.

This redefined concept of ownership also applies to the words in this book. I am the writer of these words, but believe me when I say I do not own any of the ideas found here. They are here for all of us, for all time. The moment we are ready to receive an idea, it comes to us freely. I'm not deluded enough to believe that I am the creator or owner of any of these questions or answers. I happened to be searching for answers, just like you, and attracted these ideas to me.

For business purposes in our world, you will see my name on the cover of this book. But in reality, I own nothing. Don't confuse the copyright formality with the notion that I own these ideas. The ideas here belong to neither me nor anyone else. They belong to everyone and no one. I am simply, at this time, the conduit used to convey these ideas in our human language. I relay the thoughts to you as I receive them. I am the custodian; the ideas are placed in my possession to share with you. It's that simple.

The words in this book are the gifts that my Spirit carries. In the same way, you have gifts that you carry. Our gifts are meant to be shared with the world. Our gifts are our Spiritual Wealth. As the custodians of this wealth, we are meant to nurture and share these gifts for the benefit of the world.

Henry David Thoreau once offered this valuable insight, "Most men lead lives of quiet desperation and go to the grave with the song still in them." Our gift is our song. It's in our custody right now. If we think of ourselves as owners of this gift, then we can keep it all to ourselves and take it to our grave. We can choose to do this, if that is what we wish. But if we live this way, we will feel unfulfilled and that we are living an empty life. Something will always be missing in us. Let's think of ourselves as custodians who nurture and share the wealth. Like our Financial Wealth, we experience joy when we share our Spiritual Wealth, when we let it flow.

Our gifts, our talents, are our Spiritual Wealth. As the custodians of this wealth, we are meant to nurture and share these gifts for the benefit of the world.

Before we end this conversation, I should remind you that these labels "owner" and "custodian" are just that—labels. They are words that we humans have invented to describe two specific ideas. The idea of being an owner means that we will always own something and maybe we don't necessarily have to share it with anyone. My preferred idea of being a custodian means that something is in our custody right now, for us to nurture while it is in our custody, share with others, and pass along in even better shape than when we received it. Remember, the specific words "owner" and "custodian" don't really matter. What matters is that we understand the basic concept of nurturing and sharing our wealth and letting it flow to the world.

If we each came into this world as a gifted Spirit with no possessions and we will leave with none, then we are custodians of whatever we acquire during our lives, not owners. We need not fear losing anything because we have nothing to lose. We came into the world with unique talents in our Spirit that we can never lose, regardless of our physical circumstances. So, again, we can't lose anything. This knowledge gives us a sense of courage and fearlessness. It eliminates self-doubt and worry. We can enjoy what we have, while we have it. And we can share what we have, while we have it. This is the ultimate gift.

We came with nothing but Spirit, we will leave with nothing but Spirit. We are custodians of what we acquire throughout our lives, not owners. So, what do we really have to lose?

12. WHAT IS OUR PURPOSE IN LIFE?

What is my purpose in life? This is a common question that most of us have each asked ourselves at one point or another. Deep down inside our beings, we know that we are bigger than the routine activities that we perform in our daily lives. We want more. We want our lives to mean something. We want to contribute in some significant way to the world. As such, we attempt to find out what that grand purpose for our life is. We search frantically for this all-important answer. Some of us give up the search and live meaninglessly. Others decide what their purpose is and live for it.

Parents often say they've found their reason for being when they have children. Their purpose is to be good parents and raise their children to be the best human beings that they can be. Some lucky individuals find their life purpose at a much earlier age, in a line of work to which they can devote their life. Through their work, they make meaningful contributions to the world.

Sometimes we sit back and admire our role models, such as someone who has achieved huge success in one area of life, and we believe that person must have found their purpose in life. But the fact is no one has a single purpose in life. Being a great parent or being a successful professional is never the whole picture of one life. It may be the area that is most recognized by the outside world, but it is never the entire picture.

We are complex beings with so much to offer the world. We are always much bigger than one role that we play. We may practice law, but we are more than just a lawyer. We may also be a parent, philanthropist, artist, writer, friend, mentor—the list goes on. The message here is that we have different purposes at different times in our lives. Sometimes we have more than one purpose at a given time. The bottom line is, one purpose, one label, one role, will never fully capture our entire reason for being.

As human beings, we are never satisfied. We always want more. Once the children are grown up, are out in the world on their own, and don't require the parent's constant attention, the parent has to find a new focus, a new purpose. Once we have achieved the level of success that we dreamed of in our chosen profession, the inevitable question that arises is, "Now what?"

Sometimes we become so attached to a particular role we've played for such a long time that when that chapter is over, we don't know what to do with our newfound free time. We know that change is constant, but we find it difficult to adjust to our new situation. We had a definite purpose before, and now all of a sudden we don't have one anymore. We get completely disoriented. The reason for our discomfort is that we are human. We want, or rather we need, more. It is a natural urge with which we've each been born. It is a beautiful discomfort. It is important because it keeps us alive. We always want to write that next act to our lives.

> **One purpose, one label, one role, will never fully capture our entire reason for being.**

As change is inevitable, our purpose in life cannot stay the same forever. There is never one fixed purpose for each life. Each moment carries its own meaning. This is why at different stages of our lives, we are interested in different things. Our passions change over time. So does our purpose in life. What we find intriguing today we may find boring tomorrow.

As children, our purpose may have been simply to have fun with our friends. If we go on to college, our purpose may be to make new friends, pass exams, and then, upon graduation, to find work that we love. Later when we have children, our purpose is to nurture them to become the best people they can possibly be. In our more senior years, our purpose may be to give back to society by sharing our time, money or knowledge.

Remember that, as young children at the playground, we're not thinking about college. As unwed and childless college students, the last thing on our minds is nurturing our future children. Even as our professional lives progress, we become interested in new things. As time goes on and we develop new interests, we understandably develop new meaning to our lives.

We often seek out a grand purpose and overlook real life in each simple moment. In addition to our major purpose, there is always a much simpler purpose in each moment. We sometimes get so carried away with our search for an overall grand purpose that we lose sight of the purpose in each moment. We often ignore this moment because it is a lot less exciting than the quest for a big mission statement for our life.

But life is simple and is made up of simple moments. Focusing on these simple moments is much more important than our search for grand visions and meaning for the future. There is wisdom in each moment, in simple things such as watching a movie, having breakfast, enjoying a conversation, admiring beauty, reading an inspiring quote, absorbing some interesting piece of news. There is also wisdom in everything that we feel such as joy, sorrow, anger, and even boredom. This is life. It is simple. In this simplicity lies the very wisdom that we seek in a grand life purpose.

We often consider our daily activities to be boring and routine. Well, I've got news for you—that boring and routine stuff is your life. Your life is not coming by train at some scheduled time from some faraway destination. Your life is happening right now as you read these words. Life also is not a never-ending parade with marching bands. Every moment is not glamorous. However, we do have moments in life when we enjoy the music of the parade on some special day, such as graduation day, the day we get a new job, or when we win something important. But this parade is just a slice of the bread called life. Most of life is found in the simple things that we do every day. Life doesn't announce itself with a marching band or loud bells and whistles coming down the road.

Life is here right now. We sometimes get so caught up in our future plans and purpose that we forget that life is already here. If we've never looked at life before, let's look at it today. The gift is here now.

Dreams are important because they give us the energy today to march towards a future of possibilities. But never forget that all of life lies in this moment. The seed of that dream lies in this very moment. All of our grand statements on the purpose of our life must ultimately be acted out in this simple moment. There is no date at which life starts. It is here today. It is always here today.

I'm sure we've all heard or made declarations such as: "I'll begin my new diet next month"; "Once things slow down at work, I'll sign up for the gym"; "I plan to quit smoking as of January 1"; "I hope to launch my new business in about two years"; "When I become a millionaire, I'll buy that house, and I'll be happy." The recurring theme here is that, at some later date, that new chapter in life will begin. Why not today? Why not right now?

With every dream, there is always some small thing that we can do today, right now, to bring the dream closer to us. We can always start the diet, fitness, or stop-smoking program in some small way today. There are a large number of things that the prospective business owner can do today, right now, that require little or no money to get started. By feeding this moment, we plant a seed here and now to attract the desired outcome. The prospective millionaire can be happy today, right now. The money and house are not necessary for this. They are fun toys to acquire and enjoy, but happiness, like every other emotion in nature, is absolutely free.

There is always a simple purpose to each moment. All of life lies in this moment. All of our grand statements on the purpose of our life must ultimately be acted out in this simple moment.

We make these life plans because most of us believe that we need to chase down a dream. This is one of those widely accepted beliefs that we never question. We don't need to chase anything down, we simply need to attract it to us by planting its seed today. To live our dreams, we need to spend our time in a way that will bring them to us. If we chase something, we will eventually get tired. If somehow we do catch up with it, we may realize that it is not as satisfying as it seemed from a distance.

If we find ourselves constantly chasing something elusive, chances are we may have cultivated the mindset that we need to chase it. If it is a true passion, we don't chase it; we attract each other like magnets. We can't help but live the passion in some form right now, irrespective of the external results that we produce. If we have to motivate ourselves constantly to keep doing it, to keep going, then we need to examine whether it is truly a passion.

Anything in life that is worth having is not chased down; it is attracted. For instance, if we work for someone else but are innately entrepreneurial and have dreams of owning a business, we will look to lead projects in our employer's business or run our own part-time business because we can't help it. We will not wait to own a full-time business to express our talents. By living the dream today in some form, not waiting for the so-called right time to strike out and chase the dream, we will ultimately attract the right business opportunity to us. In the same fashion, a born artist will always create here and now. If she can't afford a brush and paint today, she will dab her finger in mud and brush it across a wall until she can afford better tools for her passion.

As we chase down that dream life or search for that overall purpose to life, we are living our life. The dream doesn't bring our real life with it. Our life doesn't begin when we settle on our purpose. Life is already here. Life is here from the moment we are born.

From birth, we are tossed into specific life experiences for a reason. We were born into a specific family, at a specific location, and at a specific time in history. Everything happens as it should. As we grow up, we're guided to new places, physically, mentally, and spiritually. Our experiences shape us and guide us to future moments.

The Universe is always at work. It speaks through our Spirit to nudge us along from birth. The problems that we face in life arise when we choose not to heed the subtle nudge of our Spirit. Our Spirit guides us in big and small occurrences, pushing us to do certain things and go certain places. We often classify occurrences in our lives as either big or small; that is, this simple moment is not as important as another bigger moment. We often only notice the big things. Our Spirit doesn't discriminate between any two moments. These labels don't exist for it. Everything is equally important.

Think about a typical day in which you see people, things, and occurrences. Things happen exactly when they should. Driving to work, you could have reached that intersection in the road a few seconds before or a few seconds after you did, but you got there when you did, in order to see what you saw. You received a phone call or email at a specific time while at the office. Some planned activity got postponed for some unforeseen reason, and it finally took place at some future time. You experienced other surprises during the day. After work, you felt the urge to go out and do something, or you felt tired and sat in front of the television.

Every thought, emotion, and occurrence you experience throughout the day is there for a reason. These minor and boring things seem like simple random occurrences, but they are what makes up life. I repeat, these small things, moment to moment, make up what we call life. If we pay attention, we begin to notice that, just like in some of the bigger events in life, these smaller ones happen right when they should. They each have a purpose. They carry our wisdom within them. We just need to observe quietly our daily thoughts, emotions, and activities as often as we can. We may ignore the wisdom in this moment, but the next moment brings another message. Our Spirit is constantly feeding us these messages of wisdom to nudge us along.

Our Spirit nudges us along in big and small occurrences. It doesn't discriminate between any two occurrences. Everything is equally important.

Does this mean that our lives are planned out in advance by the Universe, and as such, we have no control over ourselves? We're each born to succeed effortlessly in life. We're born with gifts to share with the world. And we are born with a spiritual connection to the Universe. We face obstacles and attract heartache when we run away from our gifts or ignore this connection. If we follow the nudge of our Spirit, we end up reaching our full potential, which we label "success." Therefore, if we will enjoy inner and outer success by following the nudge of our Spirit, it doesn't really matter whether the path was predetermined or not.

Maybe our life path is set before we're even born. Or maybe we design our life as we move along every day. The only thing that truly matters is that we express our Spirit in the world so that we can enjoy real success. For this to happen, we need awareness of ourselves. If we can step beyond our beliefs and the noise of society in a moment, we become aware of what our Spirit wants from us in that moment, whether it is predetermined by the Universe or not. We then see past our simple societal conditioning to our bigger spiritual being. Through self-awareness, we can observe the wisdom or lack thereof in our conditioning, and our inspired actions flow naturally.

We are spiritual beings experiencing things in the physical realm. Our physical circumstances are never as big as our Spirit. Our Spirit attracts the right physical experiences that we need to express our true gifts. If we are not aware of our Spirit's quiet nudge, then we try to force things or our unconscious conditioning takes over and we blindly follow the crowd. We are born to succeed. If we can open our eyes, see beyond our conditioning, and flow with the nudge of our Spirit in each moment, we naturally and effortlessly succeed, as we should. Then, that moment has fulfilled its purpose.

Occasionally, when you're not restricted by a rigid schedule or preconceived plan, let yourself be led in small things and observe what happens. Feel what draws you naturally. By doing this, you will begin to see and appreciate the nudge of your Spirit in life's simple moments. For instance, if you enjoy reading (and I'm guessing you do), walk into a bookstore with no set idea of what you want to read and see what naturally holds your attention. Take note of the book or magazine to which you are attracted. Let your Spirit guide you. In a similar way, take a walk with no preconceived route, watch which path calls you, and note whom and what you encounter on your way.

Simple experiences like these increase our awareness of life in each moment. We begin to reconnect with that subtle nudge that attempts to guide us. Our decisions and actions become more inspired as we improve our ability to determine what is right for us in each situation. This inspiration is often referred to as "intuition." We intuitively know the purpose of the moment.

Many of us hear our intuition's voice, our Spirit talking to us, only when we have to make a big and important decision in life. We collect the necessary information and analyze the pros and cons. Then, there's that wise one within us that knows, without logical analysis, what we should do. That part of us, our intuition, our Spirit, does not discriminate between the size and importance of the decision. It doesn't care if it involves deciding whether to have a cigarette right now or deciding whether to take on that new job. They are both equally important in the grand scheme of life. Each of these two moments has its own important purpose.

The Universe is always at work in small and big things. Our daily lives are made up mostly of numerous small choices. When we are aware of this, we begin to notice our Spirit at work in our so-called simple and boring activities. This is the wisdom in the moment. This is our life, and there is purpose in each moment.

> **If we flow with the nudge of our Spirit in each moment, we naturally and effortlessly succeed, as we should. Then, that moment has fulfilled its purpose.**

Connecting with and following the nudge of our Spirit may sometimes mean that we are, in worldly terms, inconsistent. We may be one thing today and something different tomorrow. We may commit to a project today and pull the plug on it tomorrow. This is natural. If something no longer feels right, we must let it go. No two moments in life are ever identical, so why must we be consistent?

I know, the world rewards consistency. It is easier for people to label us if we are consistent in our decisions and actions. We are called "reliable" and "trustworthy." People hate surprises, so we accommodate them by playing the roles that they give us.

Sometimes we give ourselves a label and get consumed by it. The introvert is expected to always be introverted. She is not expected to get excited by a passion, and talk for days about it, like an extrovert would. The disciplined leader is always expected to be calm and in control of himself and others. He must never do anything without emotionally detached calculation and a clear and logical reason given to his troops for his decision. He can't allow himself to act crazy or follow the illogical thoughts in his gut.

These are some of the labels we give ourselves, and we die by these. But each moment calls for something unique. The well-defined label may be inappropriate for this moment. The purpose of this moment could be to act crazier or more extroverted than usual. Let's be whatever the moment calls for. If a past choice no longer feels right, let's change our mind without guilt. If our Spirit indicates subtly that we made a mistake before, let's listen to it, change direction, and be proudly inconsistent.

In order to live our purpose each step of the way, we must listen to our Spirit, and like an artist with a paintbrush, paint our life the way we want. Our Spirit guides us to our passions and interests, the way we want to live our lives. We don't need to wait for life to bring that one big answer—a life purpose—before we start living. We just need to follow our passions and our strong emotions. These lead to our purpose in each simple moment. Life is made up of each moment. Therefore, by focusing on these simple moments, we design the life we truly want.

We often need to ignore the well-meaning conventions of society in order to design our life. We can then sit down and ask ourselves what kind of lifestyle we enjoy. We must listen to those little eccentric tendencies that we have. That is where our truth lies; that is the nudge of our Spirit. Our specific unique traits are no accident. They are our authentic being.

> **We don't need to wait for life to bring that one big answer: a life purpose. We just need to follow our passions and our strong emotions. These lead to our purpose in each simple moment.**

As we follow our passions in each moment and design a life that we enjoy, let's not buy what the world is trying to sell us if it's not right for us. We mentioned earlier that the world likes to label individuals. But society also likes and needs to label whole clusters of people. It is convenient to clump people together in a group, label them, and sell them on what kind of lifestyle, as members of that group, they should be living.

This need to categorize people and sell them on how they should spend their time and money happens with every single group imaginable. We often assume that people from some of the neatly labeled economic classes—poor, middle class, upper-middle class, rich, wealthy—are inherently different from each other. Yes, their income levels may differ, but, at the core, human beings are human beings, and most people do what others in their world are doing. Each class is sold some lifestyle as the life they are supposed to have or aspire to have.

For instance, people who are deemed financially wealthy, who have attained a certain level of financial net worth, are sold the idea that they need to own certain things because everyone else in their group is buying these things, such as art, yachts, or jewelry.

For legitimate purposes, it is often necessary to take a whole group of people and throw them all in one bucket with standard characteristics, labels, and expectations. Businesses need to market their products to a group of well-defined target customers. The government needs to set tax rates for its citizens based on their income levels. Hence, these labeled groups are necessary. We can choose to live with these labels, but we must look beyond them. They shouldn't control us.

Some people purchase yachts even though they suffer from seasickness when out on any body of water. Other people have little to no artistic interest to speak of, but believe that collecting art is what they should be doing once they "make it." The more expensive the work of art, regardless of its history or beauty, the better.

We must ask ourselves if we truly love art, or the yacht, or the other things that we allegedly should have. If the answer is yes, let's acquire and enjoy them. If the answer is no, let's look elsewhere and invest our time, money, and Spirit in what we love, regardless of whether people in our position are supposed to love it.

If our idea of fun dining is chewing on a juicy hamburger at the local fast-food restaurant, then let's do it. Forget the expensive meal on a white tablecloth at that highly publicized five-star restaurant. If we'd rather go watch the latest movie at the local theater than sit through a night at the opera, let's grab a movie ticket and some popcorn and enjoy ourselves at the movies. Let's never get sucked into the hype about what we should be doing if it truly doesn't interest us. Let's do what our Spirit nudges us to do. Let's do what makes us happy.

In the professional arena, the conventional nine to five lifestyle is not for everyone. Some people are more productive much later in the day than the standard 9:00 a.m. I should disclose here that I happen to be one of those night owls who wake up in the early morning feeling miserable and exhausted. "Early to bed, early to rise" is one of those mantras that have been drilled into our heads. But it's not appropriate for everyone. Some people reach their creative peak late at night and can make no significant contribution to society during regular business hours. Does this make them lazy? Absolutely not. It is who they are.

We can't wait for the world to change its conventions. It never will, and if it does, it takes too long. Life is happening right now. Let's listen to our Spirit, and let it guide us to create our own lifestyle. If we would rather work on a park bench than in an office cubicle, this urge is within us for a purpose. We need to look into how we can design a work life to accommodate this. Let's not allow ourselves to be led astray by anyone who tells us that, by going against convention, we are being naive or unrealistic. This is our life, here and now.

We are each both the artist and the artwork. We can work on ourselves and carve out our world to our liking. That is the unique gift that we each have. The Universe introduces us into the world in a specific environment and with specific traits. The rules that society establishes are meant to facilitate the activities between its people. But a society is not made up of people with homogeneous tendencies and traits. A society consists of unique individuals. Therefore, regardless of the group into which we are expected to fall, we must design a unique life to our liking. Let's start today.

Life is inherently simple. We complicate it and attract hardship when we try to force our will, our plans, our timetables, our conditioning, onto life. We simply have to listen to the Universe when it speaks to us. Think about this: We don't plan to go to use the restroom. We don't schedule it in advance. (I don't, and I certainly hope you don't either.) We feel the urge, our body says it's time to go, and we follow its orders. "To go or not to go?" is never a question.

Our Spirit speaks to us just like our physical body does. We must listen to it and follow its quiet nudge as it presents itself in each moment of each day. Once we become aware of our Spirit in each moment, we begin to notice that everything happens when it should, and the alleged simple random occurrences begin to make sense. We see and appreciate the purpose in each moment—in the mundane moment and in the life-changing moment. To our Spirit, our guide, each of these moments is equally important.

Sometimes we are not meant to extract the wisdom in the same moment that something takes place. We may need other things to happen in order for us to look back and understand the meaning behind the chain of events. But if we watch what is happening closely in each moment, if we watch our thoughts and emotions as they pop up, in that future moment of enlightenment, we truly understand the purpose of that experience. We become wiser.

Once we become aware of our Spirit in each moment, alleged simple random occurrences begin to make sense. We see and appreciate the purpose in each moment—in the mundane moment and in the life-changing moment.

In life, we need to do what comes naturally in each moment. As we wait for the answer to the question, "What is my purpose in life?" and we work towards that dream life, let's remember that life is happening here and now. As a matter of fact, none of us is ever successful at figuring out the singular purpose of our life, because it doesn't exist. There only is a purpose for this moment. We don't know what the future holds. Our purpose lies in our current experiences. We simply need to follow the nudge of our Spirit, which presents itself in our passions, our thoughts and emotions in each moment.

Certain things arouse our curiosity at a certain moment in time: Why did it happen, and why now? We usually don't know precisely why it happened when it did. But all we need to do is follow the breadcrumbs laid out by these occurrences and see where they lead. The Universe is always hard at work.

Let's replace the idea of discovering an overall purpose for our life with something else. Instead of each of us racking our brains trying to answer the "What is my purpose in life?" question, let's live the question in each moment. All wisdom lies in this moment. Each moment brings a unique wisdom to each of us. The purpose of a moment may be to rest, take a walk, sit quietly, enjoy a meal, truly listen to the other person in conversation, be angry, be happy, be sad, or capture an insight of simple wisdom.

Today, in this moment, let's make this our purpose: To listen to the nudge of our Spirit in each moment. Add up all these moments, and you and I have what we each call "my life." So, the real question is "What is my purpose in this moment?"

Let's replace "What is my purpose in life?" with "What is my purpose in this moment?"

---

13. OUR MIND, OUR QUESTIONS—OUR LIFE

The questions we nurture in our mind bring the answers that we live in our lives. The results of our life come from the thoughts we cultivate. We can't live something if we can't see it. Our mindset attracts the life we live. We live what our mind sees.

Always remember this: We are what we become before we actually become it. To put it simply, we become it inside before everyone else eventually sees it. We think as our dream self would think, and then the dream manifests itself in reality for the rest of the world to see. We are, and then we become. The acknowledgement we receive from the outside world is always simply a final formality. We are the person we dream of before others recognize it. This may seem like putting the cart before the horse, and it is, but it is a timeless law of life.

We are, and then we become. We become it inside before everyone else eventually sees it.

It is not setting a specific goal that brings our dream to us. It is our mindset that attracts things into our life, good or bad, right or wrong. Note this: many people achieve and live things that were never explicit goals for them. The mind attracts these things. It is always working at attracting things whether we are aware or not. The wealthy mind attracts wealth. The poor mind attracts poverty.

So let's forget about chasing some fixed goal in the future. We can't control the results of life in the future. But we can control our mind right now. Beginning today, let's focus on slowly adopting the mind of the person we want to be in the future. We don't need to own whatever it is that person owns. We attract that stuff with the right mind. When faced with a challenge, let's ask ourselves, "What would that person think in this situation?" With the right mind and the right questions, the right actions flow. So let's not break into a sweat over things we can't control, such as the future. Let's channel our energies toward what we can control, such as our mind.

The mind is like a magnet. It attracts the physical equivalent of its dominating thoughts. The woman with the hundred-thousand-dollar mindset will attract hundreds of thousands of dollars. The woman with the millionaire mindset will attract million-dollar wealth. The woman with the billionaire mindset will attract billion-dollar wealth. The woman with the middle management mindset will attract the middle management job. The woman with the CEO mindset will attract the CEO job. The man with the pessimistic mindset will attract a negative life. The man with the optimistic mindset will attract a positive life. It's that simple.

Let's take advantage of this gift, this ability of our mind to attract what we want to us—this law of attraction. Instead of attracting our dreams, many of us attempt to set and chase fixed goals using widely accepted goal-setting techniques. Goals, in themselves, are not bad. As long as they don't become an obsession and take over our lives, they are good motivational tools for us. But always remember, if we have a poverty mindset, our goal of making a million dollars will almost never materialize. And if somehow it does, say we win the lottery, we will probably lose the financial wealth just as quickly as we gained it because we don't yet have the wealth mindset for it.

Once again, we never need to chase anything down. We always attract what we want by living today in the mind of the person who already has what we desire. The outside world will inevitably come around to bring our dream to us. If we desire any form of wealth—Physical, Mental, Financial or Spiritual—it should not be the goal. We should aim to acquire the appropriate wealth mindset. Then, we naturally attract the wealth we desire.

Physical, Mental, Financial or Spiritual Wealth should not be the goal. We should aim to acquire the appropriate wealth mindset. Then, we naturally attract the wealth we desire.

The questions we each ask ourselves in any given situation tell us everything we need to know about our mindset. We'll study a few minds in different scenarios throughout this chapter.

A millionaire entrepreneur who goes bankrupt almost never sees the word "employee" in his thoughts for the future. He asks himself how he can build a second fortune out of another interesting and meaningful project. His mind is built to generate these questions. Hitting the pavement in search of a regular job doesn't cross his mind. His questions are generated from an entrepreneur's mindset. On the other hand, an employee who loses his job puts together his résumé in search of a new job. His mind sees a new job in his future, and his question is, "How can I get another job?"

This concept of mindset applies to non-financial matters as well. If we ask ourselves negative questions, we get negative responses. If we ask empowering questions, we get empowering answers. The specific physical circumstances that we each live in are never the determining factors in the results of our different lives. The difference lies in the questions we each ask ourselves.

We've seen in the previous example what type of questions a typical millionaire and typical employee nurture when they each find themselves in a position in which their income sources are cut off. One could even assume that the former millionaire is in much worse financial shape than the employee, because bankruptcy could imply that he lost his assets that provided his income. The employee may simply be out of a steady paycheck and any personal assets he owned still belong to him. But to the employee, directing his energy toward coming up with ideas to create new assets and build a fortune is naive and unrealistic. To him, it just doesn't make logical sense to do that. As far as he is concerned, the only true asset he owns is the work experience carefully laid out in his résumé. Therefore, this asset is what he intends to lease out to his next employer. This is his reality.

I must emphasize here that neither one of these two mindsets is superior to the other. They are each necessary in our world. Thankfully, people are different, as they should be. The important point to note here is that we are each allotted twenty-four hours each day. The difference in the lives of any two people comes from the way each person spends their allotment of time. We each spend our time in questions—both trivial and important. We ask questions, seek answers, and make decisions as the hands on the clock tick by.

The woman who spends her time creating and building passive income-generating assets, such as businesses, will usually have more cash in the bank than the woman who gets paid by the hour for her services. The business builder may not make any significant income initially, but she is in a better position to build Financial Wealth in the future. There are only so many hours in a day. Time is limited. Receiving financial compensation solely by the hour, if we show up for work, places obvious limits on our ability to build Financial Wealth.

We each ask ourselves different questions when we find ourselves in certain circumstances. We dream and ask ourselves how we can bring that beautiful image into our lives. Note that a dream is a thought like any other thought we may have. It may carry more emotional intensity than our other thoughts, but it is still a thought. A dream is the thought of a future in which we want to live. The problem that we often face is that we have the dream, the thought, but we also counter it with images that don't help us along the path to that dream. This is the only real obstacle to us living that dream.

Think about this: If you are a successful professional, you are certain that you can quit your job and get another one somewhere else. This is a fact to you. You harbor this thought with zero doubt in your mind. This is the sole image in your mind. Guess what? You will live this thought if you do quit your job. Nothing can stop you. You can't not live this thought. After all, you see nothing else but your ability to get another job. You live what you see. Well, in the same way, the successful businessman is certain that he can build another successful business if he loses his current business.

When we doubt our ability to bring our dreams, our thoughts, to life, it is another way of saying that we ask ourselves doubt-filled questions: *Can I really do this? Am I being realistic?* It all comes back to our questions. Our questions bring our answers with them. Our answers push us to act, right or wrong. When we ask a question, we usually already have an answer within it. The way we phrase the question indicates what answer we want it to give back to us.

Look at these two questions each from two different people: "Can I really start this new business?" and "How can I go about starting this new business?" Both people have the same dream. But the second question brings the dream closer to reality than the first question. The first person has to convince himself he can do it before he explores the details of how to do it. The second person is ready to go and just needs some direction on the specifics. Both people have the ability to build businesses. But their minds generate different questions, which determine their individual results. Both of these people get twenty-four hours in each day. The first person spends his time trying to build his confidence. The second person spends his hours seeking how-to information. How they each spend their time depends on their individual mindsets.

Our mindset is overwhelmingly more important than our actual physical activity. Anyone can be busy, so we must each take the time to find out what is keeping us busy. With the right mindset, the right physical actions flow naturally from us. The right questions bring the right mindset; the right mindset brings the right questions.

Our mindset is overwhelmingly more important than our actual physical activity. With the right mindset, the right physical actions flow naturally from us.

Success in any endeavor requires very simple tools: a pen, a pad, and a mind of success. We don't need money, technology, machinery, or anything else. We can acquire all that other stuff. Frankly, even the pen and pad aren't entirely necessary, but it helps to write our thoughts down. This simple act of writing gives us clarity. But the pen and pad are useless without the mind. The mind asks questions. The mind attracts answers. Ideas abound. The mind of success is the reason why the successful person can re-create success over and over again. It's all in the mind.

Imagine that we were in search of a job. We would probably put together our résumé, do our research on prospective employers, put on our best professional attire, and go out to job interviews. We sit across a table from the interviewer, and we attempt to impress. We want to present ourselves in a way that the interviewer would like and approve of. We want the interviewer to grade our paper and tell us that we are chosen. In simple terms, throughout the interaction, our dominant internal question is, "How can I impress you?" This is the most common scenario.

Well, let's imagine another scenario in which we believe that we are qualified for the job opportunity. We clearly state and demonstrate this, but our internal question is, "How can you impress me?" With this question dominating our mind, our interview process is different. Our physical disposition changes. Our posture becomes more erect, our voice more confident, our gait more brisk.

Why should we be the only nervous party in this interaction? It's also the employer's responsibility to sell us on why we should give our precious time to his organization. It's a two-way street. We have to present our qualifications for the job, and the employer has to explain why we should choose to join his team. After all, both the employer and employee want some value out of an employment deal. Note how our attitude changes with this new mindset, with these new questions. It's pretty obvious that, in this scenario, we would project a more confident aura.

In both scenarios, we are in the exact same predicament: we need a job. The only difference is in our questions, which lead to our actions. I don't mean to imply that in the second scenario we'll definitely get the job because of our more confident mindset. Some insecure employers may find our confidence intimidating. The employer is put on the spot. The employer has to perform, too. This example simply demonstrates that, in the same situation, two different results can be produced from two different sets of questions.

In the second scenario, we project boldness and confidence that people admire and for which they secretly long. Most intelligent employers would want these qualities on their team. This bold and confident attitude is fascinating. It's a refreshing originality from the monotonous train of people-pleasing jobseekers they encounter. This wakes the employer up.

We all live in the same physical world, but we each live in a different reality. When we find ourselves in any uncertain situation, let's make a conscious effort to observe our questions. Are they negative or positive, empowering or disempowering? We act today based on the way we phrase our internal questions. We act out our answers. So it's evident that our questions today will determine our life tomorrow.

Life is uncertain. Tomorrow is unknown. So we face each moment with questions about what to do in each situation. The questions never end. That is just the nature of the journey of life. A trip from home to the grocery store ends when we get to the store. A plane ride ends when we touch down at our intended destination. A journey of self-exploration never ends.

We embarked on this journey to explore questions and seek answers. There are so many questions and so many unknowns. So much is uncertain. There is so little time. We will never know all there is to know. The answer to a question today may be incorrect for the same question tomorrow. This is a unique journey. There is no definitive insight that answers all of our past, present and future questions. There is no final destination. The journey is the destination.

The journey of self-exploration never ends. The journey is the destination.

This is the beauty of life—the never-ending quest for wisdom. There is no "there," and we're done. The wisdom we uncover on the way is all we need for that time. Unlike a mystery movie, there is no final scene where we receive some valuable piece of information, find out who the culprit is, and close the case. In this case, there is no closure. If there were, life would end. Without questions, we are certain. We are dead. We feel no emotion if we know what will happen tomorrow. Then, nothing surprises us, there is nothing more to learn. With questions, we doubt, so we explore and we discover.

In life, we embark on a new journey time and time again. We must each take on our own journey. We must each get on our own train. I can't do it for you, and you can't do it for me. As you read the words in this book, there's no need to attempt to memorize anything. Let your Spirit absorb whatever it chooses to absorb naturally, whenever it decides to do so. Your Spirit knows your Truth. My Spirit knows my Truth.

This brings to mind a great statement from Marilyn vos Savant: "To acquire knowledge, one must study; but to acquire wisdom, one must observe."

I've presented certain ideas to you throughout our conversations in this book. These ideas should generate questions in you. Some may even inspire doubt in you. Doubt is a necessary step toward enlightenment. In a nutshell, the words in this book should make you curious about yourself. We often hear, "Curiosity killed the cat." Well, I see a lot of cats and curious people all over the place, so I beg to differ. Be forever curious about your life. Observe your thoughts, your emotions, your actions, with the same curious enthusiasm of the famous detective Sherlock Holmes as he investigated clues to solve his cases. Your simple thoughts and emotions are the clues to your wisdom. This is where your wealth lies.

The other unique aspect of this journey of self-exploration is that we ultimately are headed back to our starting point. We are returning to that authentic Spirit with which we were born—that Spirit whose voice has been covered up by the noise of society. We are attempting to live authentically by listening to our Spirit.

The ultimate wealth is in living our truth irrespective of the consequences. When we start to ask questions and live authentically, we may lose friends, lose recognition, and attract pain from society. We may have to walk alone for a while. But we inevitably will attract people who are authentic, too. To live authentically requires us to get rid of the carefully crafted persona, the mask, the acceptable face we wear on the world's stage every day. Our usual audience may not like the real, authentic person. It may make them uncomfortable. The words in this book shouldn't add any new knowledge into our minds; they should remove the untruth, the mask we wear, to get to the real face, to the eternally wise Spirit with which we came into the world. The real wealth and wisdom we seek always lies within us, here and now.

So the journey is the destination, and the beginning is the end. Our wisdom is found right where it all began: inside each of us. Our authentic being holds our unique wisdom. Wisdom is in simple thoughts and emotions. All our success begins with our simple talents, our simple gifts.

We are each powerful and significant. We were born this way. This is not arrogance or misplaced self-confidence. No one is inferior or superior to anyone else. We are each the creation of a Higher Power, a power that we forever hold in our Spirit. Therefore, our questions should be empowering questions because that is who we are. Any expression of our Spirit in our work or in our personal lives is a gift to the world. Let's not be timid and settle for pieces of scrap tossed in our direction by society. Let's not waste our gift of life, our gift of time, our twenty-four hours each day, on meaningless and unworthy activities. Time is limited. But our wealthy Spirit is not. We are wealthy. We were born wealthy. Our questions should be wealthy.

The journey is the destination, and the beginning is the end. We are returning to that authentic Spirit with which we were born.

We can and should live with uncertainty. We don't need to attempt to control the future. We just need to enjoy each moment and embrace the wisdom and wealth it holds. Remember, a moment, in itself, is neutral. There is nothing special about any particular moment. A moment comes and goes, another second goes by, and life keeps trudging along. A moment becomes wise and powerful when we bring our Spirit to it.

Like a camera captures the image of a moment in time, let's capture the wisdom in a moment. It holds wisdom and wealth because we bring wisdom and wealth to it. All we have to do is ask questions about it. Let's never stop asking questions. Our life expands or contracts with the questions that we ask ourselves. When we explore our questions, we explore our wisdom, we explore our wealth, we explore our life. Our questions are a gift. Our life is a gift.

People often say, "Money makes the world go round." It is not true. Emotions rule the world. Where money is involved, emotions about money make the world go round. People do things largely out of unconscious emotional reactions to the situations in which they find themselves. Emotions are always flying around. Reason is logical, but highly unpopular.

If we can investigate our own mind, from an emotion back to the thought that caused the emotion, we will inevitably stumble upon a new insight. If we question the accepted beliefs that create the foundation of a thought and its related emotion, we will uncover wisdom and wealth hiding in plain view for everyone to see. But emotions cloud "reasonable" judgment so most of us cannot see what is right in front of us.

Moving backwards to the roots, to the foundation, of a thought and emotion, with an open mind, takes us to its simple wisdom. Once we see it, once we experience the wisdom, we are transformed forever. We are no longer the same person. Our newfound wisdom will seep into our actions, which will lift our experiences in life to a higher level. That is the wealth and wisdom in questions.

KRIS TABETANDO is a life-long student of human nature and the science of success. He is Founder and President of the publishing firm, Vonavo Media Group, whose mission is to inspire people to reconnect with their innate greatness. Kris lives in Toronto.

Visit WiseSuit.com
to share your favorite business and inspirational books with us.

www.ingramcontent.com/pod-product-compliance
Lightning Source LLC
LaVergne TN
LVHW041631070426
835507LV00008B/566